ANSWERED PRAYERS

A STORY OF GOD'S GUIDING HAND

JOSH TAYLOR

ILLUMIFY MEDIA GLOBAL
Littleton, Colorado

Published by
Illumify Media Global
www.IllumifyMedia.com
"Write. Publish. Market. *SELL!*"

Library of Congress Control Number: 2020916262

Paperback ISBN: 978-1-947360-28-0
eBook ISBN: 978-1-947360-29-7

Cover design by Michelle Denker-Sis

Printed in the United States of America

To my parents, who chose life for me.

CONTENTS

"Naked I came from my mother's womb,
And naked I shall return there,
The Lord gave and the Lord has taken away.
Blessed be the name of the Lord."

—Job 1:21

INTRODUCTION

We all hope and expect that life will go well for us. The "plan" typically includes enjoying youth, graduating from high school, attending college, securing a good job, marrying the dream girl or guy, raising a family, making a lot of money, retiring, traveling, and playing with the grandkids. Success!

Often reality tends to work against the grain of our desires. For most of us, childhood is a time of idealism and innocence. Then, in adulthood, we hit the skids. Reality can smack us between the eyes like a ballpeen hammer.

Life doesn't always work out the way we anticipate; discouragement, illness, petty conflicts, economic downturns, and business failures are all too common. These unexpected events can knock us off the path of our life plan.

I did not expect to wait until my late forties to find a wife, and I did not expect to lose her.

The following is a true story of joy, suffering, perseverance, and hope. This story illustrates God's providence in the lives of two of His creatures as He answered their prayers.

1

IDYLLIC CHILDHOOD

"In this world of give and take, there are not enough people willing to give what it takes."

—Lt. Clebe McClary

My early childhood resembled a Huck Finn existence. Deep in the southwest corner of Nebraska, my family's farm sat on a small mud river called the Stinking Water Creek. We were so far out in the boondocks that many maps didn't even show it. The Stinking Water, as we called it, resembled more of a mud creek.

The biggest town nearby was McCook, a community of a whopping 8,000 people. To us, McCook was a metropolis. Rural Hayes County was our home, with a population of less than 1,000 residents spread over 713 square miles, an area more than four and one-half times larger than the city and county of Denver. We were halfway between Denver and Omaha and without much in between except corn, cattle, and wheat.

Living out in the sticks suited my family, and life was good.

My best friend growing up was my dog named Laddy, who my parents got for me before I could walk. Laddy was a world-class hunter. He would chase whatever scent he picked up: squirrels, rabbits, raccoons. We spent a lot of time running the pastures, fields, and river bottoms, hunting and doing all a kid could dream of.

Neighbors were far and few between, so it was always a treat when I could have a day with any of my farm kid friends. Of course, that would always lead to new excursions and adventures in the wilds of the High Plains.

My dad was a hard-working farmer, and I spent many a day with him on the tractor or going places. We would go to the local livestock sale or visit a neighbor to borrow some farm equipment. In the winter, we would go to the nearby village of Hamlet and spend time at Greeley's gas station. The local farmers would come in and play rummy for a few hours before chore time. It was always good to go where Dad was going.

Mom was busy on the home front, making sure we were fed, clothed, and bathed. She worked as hard as—or harder than—my dad, and that's saying a lot. Mom never complained and was constantly on the move managing the household. Mom kept us on track.

I had three older sisters, so there was fun with them—at least fun for them at my expense. There were family gatherings with aunts, uncles, and cousins, as well as visiting nearby neighbors and church events. Life was as good as it gets, or so it seemed to me.

When I was around eight years old, my dad taught me to box, which he had learned in high school. He even owned his own set of gloves. Once he strapped the gloves on, he proceeded to punch me, landing a good jab square on the nose. My dad was not a big man, but his hands and arms were strong from farm work. That punch to the nose was one of my first experiences with pain.

Once, around the time when I was in junior high school, I

overheard my three sisters talking about life and how it could be so depressing. I couldn't relate to what they were saying. How could life be depressing? What was depression anyway? I thought life was grand. In hindsight, the lug nuts on the wheels of my life started to come off during my later years of high school and early college. I say in hindsight because it took getting through a series of difficulties before I could face certain aspects of my life that I would have rather ignored. As a junior in high school, I became a starting guard on the basketball team. This now made me one of the guys I looked up to. My life appeared great, but later in the basketball season I lost my starting position. That was a kick to my game plan's groin!

Don't get me wrong; there were a lot of great times and many fond memories from my past. But cracks started to appear in the plaster under the paint. Harsh realities started to make frontal assaults during college. I was no longer one of the popular guys like in my high school days. Multiple challenges kept creeping up.

The classes at college were more difficult and required real study time compared to anything in high school. The classes were also huge, and for me it was harder to make friends in that environment than in my hometown where I knew most everyone. And of course, it was also harder to meet girls at college than in high school. I was just one of hundreds of eighteen-year-old guys trying to figure out life in a completely alien setting.

But I learned well from my dad to keep working hard at whatever challenge was in front of me. Buck up and work through it. Just keep going. As a quote from former president Calvin Coolidge reads:

> Nothing in the world can take the place of persistence. Talent will not; nothing is more common than unsuccessful men with talent. Genius will not; unrewarded genius is

almost a proverb. Education will not; the world is full of educated derelicts. Persistence and determination alone are omnipotent.

After graduating from college, I moved to California on a whim. A hometown friend offered me a place to stay while I searched for a job. Eventually, I landed an insurance sales position in Sacramento. Starting a sales career in an unfamiliar town may not be the ideal path to success, as I quickly found out. I struggled in a mighty way; I was broke, lonely, and discouraged. The start of my professional career was a lesson in hard knocks, and struggle was a constant companion. Sometimes the struggle was intense, and hard work alone couldn't solve the problems I faced.

One weekend I found myself in what was then called Arco Arena with around 10,000 other locals at an Amway meeting. You may laugh at the thought of an Amway meeting, but it is a night I will never forget. Usually these events consisted of a host of speakers who were very successful within the Amway organization, but they sometimes included outside inspirational speakers. Lt. Clebe McClary was one of those speakers.

Lt. McClary was a great communicator with good stories, and he wore a big ole smile on his face while he spoke. I found it hard to focus on the smile with the patch over his eye and the missing arm. Nevertheless, this man told his life story. He grew up in the plantation world of South Carolina, was a star athlete, and went off to college. Life was grand. Then he enlisted in the Marines during the Vietnam War. Combat caught up with the lieutenant.

One night his platoon was under heavy fire, and Lt. McClary got blown to pieces, literally. While he recuperated in the hospital, the men of his platoon gave him a plaque that read: "In this world of give and take, there are not enough people willing to give what it takes."

Wow! That was an inspiring and humbling story to hear.

What was most moving was a passage he quoted later in his talk. It etched in my mind and has carried me through many of life's challenges since:

> [W]e . . . rejoice in our suffering because we know that suffering produces perseverance; perseverance, character; and character, hope. And hope does not disappoint us, because God has poured out his love into our hearts by the Holy Spirit, whom he has given us.

> —Romans 5:3–5 NIV

2

BETTER LATE THAN NEVER

"Most of all, I am tired of having nobody."

—Lloyd Christmas, *Dumb and Dumber*

Twenty years later, I am living in Denver, working as a financial advisor. I'm forty-six years old and single. It's April of 2007, and my buddy Nick and I had agreed to go to a singles event. Nick, one of my buddies around town, was someone I connected with for various singles events. It was always better to go to these social gatherings with a friend because you never knew what the turnout would be like. If it was less than encouraging, at least you had someone to hang out with or maybe to make an alternative plan with and depart for greener pastures. Call it strategic planning.

When I moved to Sacramento, I attended business mixers and was usually a bit uncomfortable. I tend to be more relaxed when I know someone at these "grin and grip" events.

Nick bailed at the last minute because he thought it was too expensive. I had prepaid the fee, but he had not. If I didn't go, it would be money down the drain.

Well, I was bummed that Nick cancelled. It was an all-day

event, but we were only planning to go for the evening session that included a buffet dinner and some other activities, so the fee was a bit steep considering we were only going for the later portion. At first, I figured I wouldn't go either, and then it was almost as if someone planted a thought in my brain: I'd paid the money so why not just go for the dinner, eat all I could, hang out for a while, and then head back home? On the way downtown I could run by a friend's house and pick up some bicycle parts waiting for me. I could kill two birds with one stone, which made the plan even more sensible.

When I stepped into the ballroom at the event, I looked around at the crowd for a moment and turned to leave. Maybe it was just a bad attitude on my part because the night did not go as planned, but things did not look promising.

As I turned to leave, I thought about the thirty-minute drive to get there and the price of the ticket. Why not just go pig out at the buffet before heading home? It made complete sense. Doing a one-eighty, I made a beeline for the buffet and proceeded to load up my plate and find a table. It was actually a pretty good buffet, but I was not sure it was worth the sixty-five dollars. What the heck, some return on an investment is better than a complete loss.

In hindsight, it was almost as if someone willed that I attend the event.

The tables were filling up, but I was able to find one with a few available seats and made myself welcome. The table was a mix of men and women who were not an overly interesting group. One guy was trying to be a funny man and was not succeeding. A couple people attempted to make good conversation, but most seemed totally out of place.

Since I am an introvert, diving into a group of people I do not know is not a comfortable situation for me, but I tried to chitchat with my tablemates. Mostly, I just wanted to eat as much of my sixty-five dollars' worth of food as fast as possible and call it good before I hit the road. I was sure I had room for a second and third assault on the buffet. The conversations continued at an uninteresting pace, and I again doubted my decision for the evening.

In the hubbub of attacking the buffet and finding an open table, it escaped me that the table right behind me was all women. Somehow over the years, I developed a way of looking at someone, or something, and not seeing what I was directly looking at. About ten years earlier, I started wearing glasses so I could see to drive, but those glasses were not foolproof for all circumstances. Call it looking but not seeing, or better yet visual blindness. Who knows how or when this came about, but it is not a habit that leads to winning friends and influencing people on any grand scale.

After a while several folks from my table left, including the gal sitting next to me. Suddenly, two women from the table behind me came over and joined my table, saying, "We just want to mix it up." One of the women sat in the empty seat next to me, and she was really cute and very nice. I mean really, really cute and really, really nice! I had missed seeing her when I was looking for a table—blame the visual blindness, if you will. Her name was Deborah. We started talking. Deborah made conversation easy, which was very helpful for my introverted nature.

There was a little competition, though. A guy sitting on the other side of Deborah seemed intrigued by this beauty also. To my surprise, Deborah didn't seem at all interested in him, and it took little effort to keep her attention. Soon we found ourselves alone in conversation.

After dinner, there were some raffle games in the ballroom where dinner had been held. We stayed at a table on the fringe of the activity talking by ourselves, but occasionally I ventured out into the crowd to gather more of the free raffle tickets for the evening's prizes. Deborah was content to stay at our table while I went about scavenging, thinking that maybe we could win the raffle. Mostly, we spent the next couple of hours in private conversation.

Deborah's last name was Crouse. At first, I thought she meant Krouse with a *K*, and I asked her if she was German. I come from a family that is heavily German, and anyone with a German background is of extra interest. Deborah told me her name was spelled with a *C* and actually she had very little German heritage. We laughed about that because my last name is not German, and yet I'm nearly eighty percent German.

I learned she had moved to Denver from Utah only a few years before. She worked as a dental hygienist, and her office was not very far from my office.

It is unusual for me to be able to talk to one person for an extended length of time, but Deborah was different somehow. As the evening passed, I asked her a casual question that I typically asked women I met: "So what are you doing the rest of the weekend?" She told me she was going to church in the morning. Bingo! She passed the most important test: She was a Christian.

It was turning out to be a different evening than I forecasted. Here was a really attractive and personable woman who seemed interested in me, and she was a Christian. It was like I picked the correct curtain on Monty Hall's game show *Let's Make a Deal*.

Eventually, we exchanged phone numbers. After a couple of hours chatting, Deborah decided she needed to head home. When she got ready to leave, she said somewhat emphatically, "You be sure to call me." In my forty-six years I don't recall ever having had a woman say that to me. Usually it was a struggle just to get a phone number, let alone an explicit request to call.

I remember watching Deborah walk out. She was petite, about five two and maybe 110 pounds. Her long brunette hair was beautiful. She was wearing white slacks with a pretty floral blouse and a white cardigan sweater. I can picture her walking out of the ballroom to this day. Wow!

Why didn't I walk her to her car like a gentleman? Hm, there is no good answer for that one. I think I was still in shock that we talked for so long and that she made it clear she wanted me to call her. I just sat there for about fifteen minutes without moving. I was stunned and amazed.

Finally, I pried myself out of my chair and drove home.

Nick called the next day to hear about the night. I told him I had met a really special woman.

Hopeful Beginning

Per Deborah's request, I called her that Monday. She didn't answer, so I left a message against my better judgment. To my surprise, she actually called me back a short time later, which was uncommon. This was the second time she did something that was not part of my normal experience. We chitchatted for a while and then we scheduled a lunch date.

We met that week for a nice lunch. We talked more about our backgrounds and families, and then Deborah dropped a bombshell; she was forty-eight years old and the mother of a twenty-six-year-old daughter and twenty-one-year-old son. Yikes! I couldn't believe it. I would have bet she wasn't a shade over thirty-eight, let alone older than me.

I always thought I wanted to have kids, but there was no way a forty-eight-year-old woman was going to have more kids. I was the youngest of four siblings, and for whatever reasons, none of my older sisters could have kids, so there was some expectation that I would carry on the family gene pool.

Deborah was so charming I put aside my personal goals, and we scheduled a second date.

Two years earlier I began visiting a counselor to work through some personal challenges. My counselor, Rick, endeavored to convince me that having kids was not all it was cracked up to be. Yes, kids could be tremendously rewarding, but they could also be nightmares. That made me think about the nightmare I was for my parents at times—maybe too much of the time. Would I want me as a child? That gave me chills.

Also, I was getting to an age that having kids would create other challenges. As I got older, I just figured I would buy a ton of life insurance, so when I died old with young kids the missus and the kids would live well, and the kids could get through college.

Regardless, I kept Rick's words in the back of my mind as Deborah and I continued to see each other.

The Second Date

A few years prior to this, my mom had knee replacement surgery that went awry, so now my sisters and I brought her to see a knee replacement specialist in Denver. I was standing behind the doc as he sat looking over the new X-ray of my mom's knee. Even this redneck farm kid could see the knee parts were off-kilter. I said, "Doc, that doesn't look right." He mumbled something but saw the same thing I did.

The doctor's final analysis was that Mom needed a complete replacement of the first knee replacement. A knee re-replacement is a pretty traumatic event for the body, and my mom was in her mid-seventies.

Her surgery was scheduled in Denver, so she could stay with me throughout her recovery. There was a conflict, though; Deborah and I scheduled our second date on the same day as Mom's surgery. Ultimately, I developed a game plan to hang out with Mom at the hospital, meet Deborah for an early date, and then pick up Mom in the evening.

Well, I was in seventh heaven on my date with Deborah, and I kept finding ways to extend it. First, we went to the Ben Franklin exhibit at the Museum of Natural History. We both liked history, and the exhibit was very interesting. We took our time walking through the exhibits and reading the interesting tidbits about old Ben. Now and then we would get slightly separated while looking at different exhibits, but I always kept my eye on her—I was curious about what she found most interesting and curious about what made her tick.

After the museum we went to dinner. We sat there for a long time grazing and talking. Being with her made me chatty, which wasn't normal. Toward the end of dinner I convinced Deborah that we should go to a movie. I really didn't want the night to end. Of course, Deborah kept asking about my mom. She seemed more concerned about her than I was.

We saw a lighthearted comedy. Later I learned that Deborah was a big-time movie buff with a large library of the old classics from the 1930s, '40s, and '50s. The goofy movie I chose was not the type of movie she would have selected. Deborah's idea of a good movie was along the lines of *Citizen Kane*, whereas I preferred movies like *Dumb and Dumber*.

She likely rolled her eyes during the whole show and regretted her decision to give me her phone number. I had a lot to learn.

The movie ended about 9:00 p.m., and I accepted the date was over. I made it to the hospital sometime after 9:30 p.m. The recovery and discharge room were closed, and they had moved my mom to a side room. They actually set her up in an unused hospital room, which was very thoughtful of them. I am sure they thought I was some kind of orc, but what the heck! A man has to do what a man has to do.

Though I love my mother, I was much more focused on Deborah at that moment. I enjoyed one of the best dates of all time, and my mom seemed happy for me. I believe that was an answer to one of her prayers.

3

YOU'RE THE ONE FOR ME!

"To find a prince, you gotta kiss some toads."

—Foxy Brown

The week after our first date, I was in charge of a big bicycle race called the Wheels of Thunder Classic. Organizing a bike race takes a lot of time. There are months of advance planning, and the closer you get to race day the more time it takes and the more stressful life becomes.

You have to coordinate with county officials, sheriff's departments, and fire and rescue squads in order to close major roadways. You have to coordinate a large pack of volunteers, which adds up to a considerable task. The week of the race leaves little time for anything else, and I did not call Deborah for the better part of that week.

The only day that worked for lunch the following week for Deborah was Tuesday. Normally, I attended a Bible study during Tuesday lunches, but I skipped it to be with her. As we sat there talking after lunch, Deborah whipped out some dental floss right at the table and began flossing her teeth. That caught me somewhere between being shocked and amused, but then again, I had never dined with a dental hygienist before.

As we left the restaurant, Deborah was kind of skipping away almost like a high school cheerleader. Looking back over her shoulder, she said, "Call me if you have time."

Ah, of course, I told her I would.

The next weekend was the three-day Memorial weekend. I typically headed back to the farm taking extra time off to see friends who were back for my high school's annual alumni banquet and to do maintenance around the farmstead. This year, my middle sister flew in from Tucson to drive back with me.

After my dad died, I had become the manager of the farm and went back often to help my mom with an assortment of tasks that needed to be done around the farm. I'd help tear out old trees, repair fences, and work on buildings. Holidays and long weekends were a good excuse to get out of Denver for an extended period and gave me an opportunity for pheasant hunting in the fall. I liked living in Denver, but I needed my breaks from the hustle and bustle of city living. These long weekend getaways to the farm were perfect stress relievers.

Most people in metro Denver head west up into the high country of the Colorado Rockies for their summer vacation weekends. Not me! I'd head east to the high plains of western Nebraska—where the heat and humidity are like long-lost cousins you'd prefer not to cross paths with and where the wind roams about like a mad cow.

Deborah, as far as I knew, was staying in Denver and hanging out with friends that weekend.

Our next date was scheduled a week later when we headed to a rustic restaurant hidden in the foothills of the Rockies about forty minutes west of Denver. Deborah had never been there, and I thought a drive to an out-of-the-way place up in the mountains would make for a fun evening. I'm not so sure Deborah was as enthused as I was though. She was more of a city girl, and rustic really wasn't her thing—nor was camping —so our next dinner date was at a slightly more sophisticated place.

During that time, I was in the process of buying a new vehicle. In the meantime I drove my old Pathfinder, which was in good condition except for a switch on the console that was bad. If the switch wasn't working, I couldn't shift into drive. You know, if you wanted to drive somewhere, being able to shift it into gear is kind of important.

While waiting for the new switch, I learned from a mechanic that in the short-term I could pop off a really small cap on the console, insert a screwdriver, and get the car to shift into drive. Problem solved.

On one date with Deborah, I proceeded to pull out my long, thin, rusty screwdriver and inserted it into the hole in the console. With the screwdriver protruding straight out of the console about six inches, Deborah asked what I was doing. After I explained the situation, she shook her head and said, "That is something my dad would have done." I took that as a nice compliment.

Deborah was capturing my mind and soul. It seemed as though she was really interested in me, and I was having a hard time believing a woman as charming and beautiful as her could like me that much.

And then I almost dropped the ball.

So Much to Learn

Life had become really busy. I was involved in leadership with the local branch of the International Christian Cycling Club, and several more events were on the schedule besides the Wheels of Thunder Classic bike race. There was our volunteer work at Elephant Rock, which is a massive one-day community ride in June. Then came our fund-raiser bicycle ride called Pedal4APurpose in July, and we had to plan for the 24 Hours of Moab mountain bike race in Utah in October. All of which meant more meetings and time devoted to planning and organizing.

I really wasn't aware of how much time I was spending with my volunteer duties or how my duties had increased, almost like the proverbial frog slowly being boiled in a pot.

During the summer I also traveled to California to see old friends, went on a wild and dangerous raft trip down the Royal Gorge, enjoyed some bike riding events, and went on another trip to the farm over the long Fourth of July weekend.

Time whisked by like a horsefly. I lost track of the days and neglected to talk to Deborah for some time. During that time, she changed jobs. Her new office was way up in north Denver, which put a crimp on our lunch dates. Of course, I was bummed that she was not close to my office anymore, but I still had no excuse to not see her for almost a month.

One evening after the Fourth of July, I called Deborah. After catching up she said emphatically, "I haven't seen you in over a month!" Her voice held a tinge of anger, frustration, desperation, and exasperation all wrapped together. Uh oh!

I went into a slight panic mode when I heard her voice and words. Several thoughts flashed through my mind. First, never ever in my life had any woman ever complained about not hearing from me, and that told me she seriously liked me. Second, I realized we hadn't scheduled a date in some time. And finally, I thought I may have blown it, and she would say adios.

I may be slow, but I'm not stupid. As quickly as I could, I gathered up the marbles still remaining in my brain and scheduled a date with her. We went bowling that following Saturday. Deborah and Mike, her son, really enjoyed bowling together, and they spent many days at the bowling alleys. They liked bowling so much they each owned their own custom bowling ball and shoes. Bowling for them was a low-key way to hang out together.

Deborah and I enjoyed a great time that night. Deborah's spunky personality was captivating, and whether she knew it or not she hooked me like a master angler. That was the night she reeled me in, and I became attached to her. That was the night my life started to change.

From that day forward, I made sure to call her more often, and she even taught me how to use my cell phone to text her, which was an excellent way to stay in touch.

Now we were talking often each week, and I texted her almost every morning.

The Saturday after the bowling night was my birthday, and I had already scheduled a weekend mountain bike trip with Rich, my best buddy in Denver. We were going to Monarch Crest Trial, and thus I was going to be out of town again.

Deborah was unhappy with me for not telling her about my birthday sooner. The weekend after my bike trip, she came to my house to barbeque and to celebrate my birthday, belatedly. We had a great evening together, and after the BBQ and desert we watched some old movies.

The next weekend I was out of town again. This time it was for a family event in Tucson. It seemed that I held the travel schedule of a rock star that year, and Deborah was getting frustrated with me. We needed to spend time together.

We spent the last Saturday night in August together, and then I was off with Rich for another mountain biking trip—this time to Durango for the Yeti Tribe Fest Mountain Biking Festival. After the big Saturday ride, there was dinner and then an evening bonfire. While standing around watching the flames, I met a couple from my area of Nebraska. Small world!

These mountain biking trips were all scheduled before I met Deborah. They were boatloads of fun, but I really wanted to be back in Denver with her. She had reeled me in that night bowling back in July, and all I could think about was spending time together.

One weekday in late summer, Deborah got off work early,

so I left the office and ran out to her condo. We headed up into the foothills for a hike followed by dinner and a movie. It was the best of times when we were together.

Soon my schedule started to return to normal, and our relationship progressed rapidly from that point. We were finding more ways to spend time together. We went to church, had dinner out, met friends for dinner or barbeques, or just watched a movie. The fall of 2007 was a fabulous time with Deborah.

Little did I know that Deborah missed me as much I missed her when we were not together.

In fall 2017, Deborah received some thrilling news that Dainah, her daughter, was going to have a baby. Deborah was going to be a grandmother twenty-six years after becoming a mother herself. As excited as she was, she was also not feeling well. She had some sort of flu bug she could not kick even after being on an antibiotic for ten days, which made her cranky and irritable. Also, her sinusitis acted up often, which did not help. I could relate to Deborah being irritable, as I am not fun to be around either when I'm sick. In fact, I'm pretty much a big wimp when I'm sick, and my grumpy German genes often kick in.

We had a date scheduled though she was still suffering flu-like symptoms. I decided unilaterally that she should stay home for the evening. I thought I was doing her a favor, but instead, I really hurt her feelings—so much so, she was ready to give me the boot. Once she told me this, I apologized profusely.

Meeting the Family

One Saturday night in October, my brother-in-law came to town briefly and stayed with me. He was the first member of my family to meet Deborah. The three of us headed out for dinner. While waiting for our food to arrive, Deborah accidentally knocked over her big glass of iced tea, flooded the table, and partially soaked my brother-in-law's jeans. She was extremely embarrassed. She thought that once word got back to my family about the tea-tipping incident they would hate her. How wrong she would be.

Upon returning to my house, Deborah was still apologizing and then my brother-in-law gave her a big hug. I couldn't believe what I was witnessing. I don't think I'd ever seen him give anyone a hug, including my sister, and here he was hugging Deborah to comfort her. Once again, in the back of my mind, I knew this girl was special.

We made plans for Deborah to come home with me for Thanksgiving to meet the rest of my family. The weekend before Thanksgiving, my good friends Tim and Theresa came to visit.

Deborah and I enjoyed their company. While out and about with them, we visited a pottery store that sold neat cookie jars in the shape of dogs. Deborah loved dogs and grieved having to give her dog to another person when she moved. In the store, Deborah pouted about never having a dog again. Instantly an idea popped into my head. I promised her that someday she would own a dog again and then slipped away from Deborah and Theresa as though I were browsing another part of the store. I snuck up to the cashier to pay for the pottery cookie jar dog, and I arranged to come back in a few weeks to pick it up. That was going to be Deborah's surprise Christmas present.

Later that week, Deborah and I drove to Nebraska for Thanksgiving with my family. It was the first trip to the farm for Deborah. Later in the evening, after Deborah had left the living room to get ready for bed, my mom said, "She seems like a really nice girl." In my opinion, she was the nicest girl.

It was a short Thanksgiving trip to Nebraska as we had to return to Denver for the annual Nebraska-Colorado football game, which was on the Friday after Thanksgiving that year.

Tim and I were going to meet some friends at the game. I was eager for friends from near and far to meet Deborah. On the way back, we stopped in Fort Morgan to visit briefly with my aunt, uncle, and cousins.

Good thing it was a quick trip. Taking someone home to meet the parents for the first time was a challenge for everyone, and making it an extended stay would have added to the complexity. Deborah was always very personable and engaging with all my family and friends, and, of course, everyone liked her instantly.

Because of her charm and ease around new people, I thought she was an extrovert. Only much later would I come to understand Deborah was more of an introvert and my thrusting her into all of these new social situations was building up a dam of pressure that was about ready to blow. I was clueless as to how much stress and anxiety I was causing her by dragging her from one place to the next to meet new people during our Thanksgiving trip.

Soon after, Deborah and I experienced our first fight while at dinner. I was flummoxed! It came out of nowhere, for seemingly no reason. I did not know what to do. Deborah wanted me to take her home early.

Well, I needed some emergency help, so after dropping off Deborah, I called Theresa for some female advice. I explained the situation as I saw it and then listened to her all the way home. Theresa was always ready to talk, and she tried to provide some insights as to what might have happened from Deborah's perspective. In the end, I was still confused.

Deborah thought we were through, but she called the next day to apologize anyway. She asked for a second chance, but she didn't have to. I was already sold out for her.

When we got together again a few days later, I still didn't know what caused the fight. I just know that I was relieved that life was back to normal for us.

Turning Point

December was another fun month as we continued to spend more time together and went to several Christmas events. We even enjoyed Christmas shopping together. A highlight was going to the play *White Christmas* at the Buell Theater. Deborah was a fan of classic movies and I was a fan of almost all Christmas movies, so seeing *White Christmas* live was a thrill for both of us.

We were invited to a Christmas party with a number of mutual friends. It was a fun and relaxing afternoon. The ladies worked on making Christmas ornaments at the party, and I remember looking at Deborah thinking how cute she was as she focused on her ornament. It was turning out to be a grand Christmas season, one of the best ever for me.

A few days before Christmas, Deborah and I had dinner together and watched a movie. The next morning Deborah headed to Utah to her mom's, and I headed to Nebraska to be with my family. I was lonely without her.

The Saturday after Christmas, some of my close friends from back home were in Denver and wanted to connect with us. Deborah and I planned to spend the afternoon with them. At dinner, someone ordered top-shelf margaritas. Deborah was not one to drink alcohol; in fact, I don't think she had had a drink in years, which should have been a red flag when the margaritas were ordered.

I was busy chatting with my old friends, and before I realized what was happening, Deborah was on her second margarita. Of course, the margaritas were really smooth, and I don't think Deborah was remotely aware of the punch they packed.

It was a festive dinner with lots of chatter and laughing. When we got up to leave and say our goodbyes, I noticed that Deborah was a little weak in the knees, and I held on to her as we walked to the truck.

On the way home, Deborah started to get sick. By the time we got to her house, she was really sick, so sick I considered taking her to the hospital. After several hours, the worst was over. I held Deborah in my arms, making sure she would be okay, and she looked up at me with her beautiful, brown, bloodshot eyes and mumbled, "I love you."

I was now forty-seven years old and never in my life had a woman ever said that to me. When she said those words, I knew in the back of my mind that I would marry this girl.

The next day I asked Deborah if she remembered what she told me the night before. She didn't, so I told her. And then I told her I loved her as well. Little did I know how much that meant to her, that it was an answer to her prayers.

That New Year's brought a whole new meaning to life for us.

Not only was she a fan of old movies but she loved music, and country music was at the top of her list. She owned a lot of George Straight music and talked often of seeing him in concert. Brad Paisley was another favorite, and he was scheduled to be in town, so I surprised her and bought tickets to his concert. Deborah was very excited and bragged to her friends at work. It was one of the coldest nights in Denver that winter, but it was worth the trip downtown for the concert and the time together.

Then came our first Valentine's Day. I picked Deborah up, and we went out for dinner. Of course, I met her with a dozen red roses. Later in the evening she gave me a card:

You're the One for Me
There I was—
one minute getting to know you,
enjoying you, and wondering
where it would all lead . . .
and the next,
thinking about you all the time,
knowing that I never, ever
wanted to be without you!
I guess that's the way life is.
You're going along,
doing your everyday things,
and out of the blue,
life gives you this wonderful present,
a present you had no idea
how much you wanted.
That's what you are to me, you know,
a precious gift.
Falling in love with you
was something I hadn't expected,
but being in love with you
is something I couldn't stop,
even if I tried.
What I'm trying to say is—
you're "it" for me,
now and forever (L. Elrod)

Happy Valentine's Day!

Love, Deb

Over the years, I rarely had a date on Valentine's Day. I usually managed to miss out on the big night. Not this time. It was a wonderful night, and Deborah made all those past frustrating Valentine's Day memories fade away. My prayers seemed to be answered.

4

TRIFECTA

"Never, never, never give up."

—Winston Churchill

March 3 was Deborah's birthday, but she did not know that I knew it was her birthday. She was upset with me for not telling her about my birthday sooner, and her revenge was not to tell me her date of birth. However, playing Colombo, I snuck a peek at her driver's license once when the opportunity was available while she was getting ready for one of our dates. Unbeknownst to her, I obtained the secret data. I wanted to make her birthday special, so I hatched my plan.

I ordered a flower delivery to her office, catching her by surprise. They were a big hit, so much so I got an immediate call from her. The flowers were delivered with a note:

Dear Deb,
Gotcha! Happy Birthday!
Love, Josh

Later she told me that her coworkers referred to me as the

"flower guy." After work we headed out to dinner for an impromptu birthday celebration. Besides the flowers, I also gave her some gift cards for massages to help her deal with the physical pain due to her many years as a dental hygienist. I thought massages might help her get some relief for her tense and sore muscles.

We decided to start taking some country dancing lessons. I had taken lessons periodically over the years but still had only a rudimentary skill level. Dance class was another way to get together on a regular basis. We discovered beginning dance classes at the Stampede Saloon. It was always a fun time, but it didn't take long for Deborah to learn I was tone deaf.

During the classes, the teachers showed us how to execute a dance step while everyone observed. Then we would couple-up to practice, first without music and then with music playing. Toward the last part of each class, our teachers would queue up the music and everyone would practice what they learned while the teachers watched, gave hints, and answered questions.

At one of these lessons, in the last phase of the class, Deborah and I were going around the dance floor practicing when she said, "You are off the beat." So we stopped, reset ourselves and took off again. Not even making it around the dance floor, she once more said, "You are off the beat again."

I had no clue what she was talking about and asked, "What do you mean 'the beat'?"

She just rolled her eyes and asked, "Can't you hear the beat?"

"What do you mean?" I replied.

It was there that she learned she was dating someone with nearly zero musical aptitude. I had taken guitar lessons as a kid, at great expense to my parents, and to this day I own a candy apple red electric Fender guitar. Yet, I have no clue how to play since none of the lessons stuck. Though I thought I wanted to play, the lessons and practicing were difficult, and even my guitar teacher would get frustrated. Heck, I can't even sing and clap my hands at church at the same time; I can do one at a time, but not both or everything goes haywire.

I'm sure it was tough for her. She loved music. She grew up playing the violin and in high school was involved with All-State Choir, a cappella choir, and the madrigal group. So not only was my choice of movies disturbing for her, but now she realized I was musically challenged, too. Thankfully, she did not dump me over that transgression, though I was down to one strike left.

That third strike would have come if I still had my crooked teeth. In fact, I probably wouldn't have even gotten her number if it hadn't been for my braces, which I got off, thankfully, just a few months before I met her. Deborah was kind of a dental snob. She was insisting that she be the one to clean my teeth and not just twice a year but each quarter. So I made the trip up to her office for my quarterly cleanings.

One time, after she finished cleaning my teeth, I told her, "You know, if not for my braces before we met, I bet you would not have gone out with me very long, or you might not have even given me your number." She, of course, denied that she would have done that. But once when her daughter visited, I brought up the subject, and Dainah confirmed I would not have lasted long with Deborah with a bad set of chompers. At that point Deborah didn't have much to say, and Dainah and I lightly chuckled about having cornered her on her dental snobbery.

The braces prevented strike three long before I knew I would be in such a tenuous situation. As they say, "God works in mysterious ways."

I also eventually learned she did not like seafood. Neighbors down the street were having their annual Cajun barbeque that included fresh crawfish flown in live from the crawfish factory, wherever that might be. They invited us to stop by. The party was being held in the garage and driveway. Deborah was appalled at the sight of the live crawdads in the big bag, and the cooking and the smell. She wanted to leave immediately. I convinced her to stay for a while and found her something else to eat.

Deborah would only eat beef, chicken, or pork. Not only was fish out of the equation, but so was any form of wild game. Her dad was a big-time outdoorsman, hunter, and fisherman. Growing up she was dragged along (her words) on multiple camping trips that included fishing and hunting excursions, and her dad supplied a lot of the meat for the family through his outdoor skills. Deborah loved her dad, but for whatever reason fish and game did not sit well with her. Hence, she developed a distaste for all these phenomenal sources of protein. Needless to say, I adjusted.

We made a trip to Utah that spring to see Mike, Deborah's son, who had moved back to Salt Lake City. He decided that since his mom and I were serious, his mom did not need him around anymore to watch over her. Deborah's view was that it was time for him to fly the coop and become a man, spreading his wings, as they say. Funny how he felt he watched over and protected by his mom, and Deborah thought she was watching over and protecting him.

Most of Mike's old high school buddies were in the Salt Lake City area, so it made sense to head there to find work. Deborah really missed Mike. They had an extremely close relationship, but she also knew he needed to leave her and go out on his own.

On the way to Mike's, we stopped and visited Deborah's brother, Steve, and his family. It was my first trip to Price, Utah. The next day it was on to Salt Lake City to have dinner with Mike and then over to stay the night with Becky, Deborah's friend from her time living there. Becky and Deborah worked together in a dental office and had become best girlfriends.

It was good for Deborah to spend some time with Becky.

In her short time in Denver she worked in several offices and made many friends, but then would be off to a new job and none of her friendships really stuck. She did not have the opportunity to build that really important relationship like she enjoyed with Becky.

One of my good friends, Cynthia, especially adored Deborah. Everyone that I introduced Deborah to instantly liked her, and it was the same with Cynthia. Knowing Deborah's deep desire for some female companionship I asked Cynthia to make sure to invite her to any girl's activities she planned. Cynthia was more than happy to do so.

After we got back from Utah, Deborah's excitement level was increasing daily. Dainah was about to give birth, and Deborah was reminiscing about when Dainah was born. Now she was going to have a grandbaby! Our plan was to fly to Indianapolis after the baby was born and spend a few days.

Isabela Grace was born on April 3, and we planned our trip a few weeks later. Deborah was really jazzed to take the trip together—her meeting her new grandbaby and me meeting her daughter. It was a huge deal for me to be along for the visit.

Then tragedy struck.

I had been running around most of Sunday and not turned on my cell phone until late in the day. I had a voice mail from my close friend Rich with a message that his newborn died at the hospital. He was only eleven days old, just a few days younger than Isabela.

Of course, I was in a state of panic once I heard the news. I called Rich and Deahna and headed over to their house. On my way, I frantically called Deborah and gave her the news; without thinking, I told her I would not be able to go to Indy.

All that could go wrong went wrong.

My best friend's baby boy died. Then Deborah took my call to mean that she and her family were not important. In her mind, she was ready to give me the boot; our relationship was over. She was devastated that I was not going with her. Her joy was seriously hurt. It was a no-win situation.

Well, as hurt as Deborah was, she thankfully did not give me the boot, and I took her to the airport that Thursday and stayed behind for the funeral in Denver. Through all of this I got hit with a severe case of the flu. It was a rough weekend.

More New Territory

All relationships are bound to have problems, and it was no different for Deborah and me. Usually, I thought our intense discussions were good for us, that we were working through our problems and getting them out in the open so they could be debated and resolved. But for Deborah most of these discussions seemed like full-blown fights and often left her feeling hurt, frustrated, and angry.

As mentioned earlier, I had started counseling about two years before I met Deborah. I was frustrated with parts of my life, and at age forty-five I decided to take some action, set my ego and arrogance aside, and get some help. Actually, what prompted my pursuit of counseling was channel surfing. Yup, channel surfing. Any normal American male understands the value of channel surfing on the old boob tube. One night when I was practicing my surfing skills, I landed on one of the church channels I watched on occasion.

That night a local preacher was on the tube. He was a guy I didn't much care for. He had slicked back hair and super expensive suits, and he wore a different one each time he was on television. I had developed a bad attitude about this particular televangelist and was always curious what nutty thing he would say next.

As he appeared on the television screen the words out of his mouth were, "If you are struggling in an area of your life, then get some professional help." That's all I heard, and I turned off the TV. His words struck me like when Dad punched me in the nose trying to teach me to box as a little kid. Pow!

In that one instant I knew I needed to start getting some professional advice on a personal level.

Why not? I'm a Certified Financial Planner™ and an insurance advisor. People ask me to help them in areas of life in which they are not proficient, such as their insurance, investments, and financial planning needs. It would be arrogant to assume that there were no areas in my life in which I also may need professional help. But arrogant I had been, or, at the minimum, ignorant. Whichever it was, arrogance or ignorance, my eyes started to open.

The next day I asked my Bible study teacher if he knew of any counselors. He gave me some names, and one of them, Rick, returned my call, so we set an appointment.

Through counseling I confronted parts of myself that were not pleasant, even somewhat depressing. Every one of us wants to believe we are a good person and are okay. But I also think deep down we know we have faults, sometimes glaring ones. Going to a professional of any type, whether a CPA, attorney, psychologist, or physician, requires that you dig deep into the matter at hand. It is especially difficult to do this when it comes to facing who you are as a person—the core of what makes you tick.

One revelation that eventually came out of my counseling was an anxiety problem. That kind of blew me away as what I was experiencing was not what I thought anxiety was. But after thinking about some patterns in my life, it started to make sense. It was not the kind of anxiety that was paralyzing or required medication, but it certainly could mess with me in social situations.

One such situation happened when Deborah and I visited her old church. You see, when we started dating, she started attending Cherry Hills Community Church where I was a member. She had been going to Ken Caryl Baptist Church for a couple of years and really liked the church and their pastor, so one Sunday we decided to go there for church. For reasons I don't understand and can't explain, as we approached the church my anxiety kicked in big time. I was out of my comfort zone and internally very nervous. It was no one's fault at the church; I just felt anxious. And to make matters worse Deborah trotted us all the way down front to sit, which did not help my state of mind one bit.

Of course, after the service I did not make a good impression with a couple of Deborah's friends, one being the pastor's wife. Afterwards Deborah was as angry as a rattlesnake with me, and the day went completely downhill from there. We didn't talk much the following week. I felt so bad that I sent Deborah an apology letter. She sent me a reply letter, which helped.

We agreed to have lunch on Sunday, which was Mother's Day. It was a beautiful spring day. I arrived first, and as Deborah walked up to the door, I knew deep down inside that she was the one for me and that we needed to find a way to work through our struggles.

We asked for a table outside. I think we were both nervous, but we talked and enjoyed a good lunch, went for a walk, ate some ice cream, and spent the rest of the day together. It ended up being a fantastic day, and our relationship seemed good again.

The coming Saturday was the big annual bike race, and I did not see or talk to her all week. But Sunday Deborah came over, and, wanting to get out of the house, we went driving around casually looking at new houses. We didn't talk about marriage, but I think she, like me, knew in the back of her mind where we were heading. We had dated seriously for more than a year, and all the signs were leading us toward hitchin' the wagon.

Deborah began having some female health issues that were causing her a lot of physical pain. The doctor recommended surgery, but Deborah did not have sick pay or a disability plan, and she had no clue how she could afford to take time off from work for the required recovery. In the midst of this news, her back and neck were still giving her fits and her sinusitis made regular visits. I knew the girl was hurting, but it was hard for me to understand the intensity and how exhausting it was for her.

Then, we had another argument. This time I knew I was out of line. So I sent her another letter letting her know how important she was to me and apologizing for hurting her. I also told her I would not call her for a few days as all I was doing was causing her grief.

Deborah wrote me a letter back expressing that I was forgiven. She also explained who she was and what some of her needs were as a woman. That also helped. It was encouraging to read her words, and it always made me feel good to know she forgave me. Forgiveness is a priceless gift.

Then before you knew it, Memorial Day weekend was upon us, which meant another trip to the farm. Getting in the car and hitting the open road, for whatever reason, calmed the tension between us.

There was farm work to get done, my annual high school alumni banquet, and the Memorial Day service and lunch. Deborah really enjoyed going to the farm. She liked the solitude and quietness. It was a good getaway from Denver, and Deborah and my mom enjoyed time together.

Every now and then, we would have another fight, so eventually Deborah asked me if I would consider going to counseling together. I was all for it. I experienced the benefit of therapy personally and felt it would help us deal with our struggles constructively. Since we were getting very serious, it made complete sense to work on our relationship before we made a major commitment to each other.

My therapist referred us to his female office partner,

Kenna. Deborah felt completely comfortable with Kenna, but for some reason she was also scared.

Deborah came to believe that the farm, my friends, the bike races, and bike riding were more important to me than her. She felt as though she were last on my long list of stuff. That was not my intention, but over the years I certainly had piled up my commitments. I guess I did not realize how time-consuming they were. Deborah pointed out this dynamic to me one night during a telephone conversation, and finally, the light bulb in my brain clicked on. I started to understand how she felt and how much time I was devoting to things other than her. From that point on, I started to make adjustments and to disengage from a number of activities.

A few weeks later, Rich and Deahna's annual raft trip was on the schedule. That year the group headed to Buena Vista down the infamous Numbers section of the Arkansas River. The Numbers is one of Colorado's most famous rafting sections, which includes some Class V rapids. Deborah was not interested in being on or in the water, so I went by myself.

It was a fast, crazy trip. We left Friday night and had a big day on the river. The water was ice cold and churning like a blender. After a few hours in the rapids, my energy was zapped. Then, we had a long drive back to Denver. I was completely exhausted by the time we made it back to town.

Friends of ours were having a party that night, and Deborah and Cynthia went together. I was to meet them there to pick up Deborah. By the time I made it to the party, I was wiped-out and irritable. I heard about some other friends getting engaged, and that made me even grumpier. I just wanted to get home, take a hot shower, and go to bed.

After leaving the party, I cantankerously babbled about looking for rings, saying something like, "We are probably going to get married, so we better get on with it." Deborah was stunned at my bluntness. In my state of fatigue, I didn't know what I was saying. Yet, now that the cat was out of the bag, so we did have to get on with it. We later laughed about this on more than one occasion.

Now we were moving fast. We did more house shopping and shopped for a ring. In June, we put a security deposit down on a new house. We picked a lot that already had the basement dug out, and the crew was ready to frame the walls. The design included a walkout basement that backed up to open space, which we both loved, and a double-deep two-car garage, which immediately got me thinking of the workshop I could put together. It was going to be Deborah's dream house. We were excited.

On a sunny, warm Sunday in late June (my dad's birthday to be exact), we went out to the lot. In what was to be the basement of our future house, I kneeled in the dirt and officially asked Deborah to marry me. She accepted.

God does answer prayers.

We continued counseling together with Kenna. Sometimes Deborah attended her own session with Kenna, and I attended my own with Rick. It was tough facing some of our individual struggles, let alone learning how those struggles affected our relationship together. But anything worth having is worth working for.

Kenna guided us through a relationship workbook. There were twelve chapters, and each took a fair amount of self-study to complete. Each chapter made you dive deeper into your past and who you were as a person: your childhood, wounds, fears, joys, hopes, goals, and more.

Jeff at the jewelry store showed us a number of rings. Nothing really caught Deborah's eye. Then he had an idea. He showed Deborah a loose diamond, and she loved it. Because of some of her allergies she could not have a gold band, so he explained how they could have a custom palladium ring made in which to mount the diamond. She was sold.

For the first time in my life I was buying a ring for my bride to be, and I couldn't believe how expensive the dang thing was. Nobody told me about this part of the deal. Yikes! Back in the day redneck farm kids in Nebraska grew up understanding extra cash was for tractors, combines, and cattle, not for frivolous objects like jewelry and houses. But I overcame my early childhood programming. I thought, "This is the only ring I'll ever buy, so I need to spend whatever it takes to make Deborah happy."

When the ring was ready, Deborah cried tears of happiness the first time she tried it on. It really was a beautiful ring. Not extravagant, just beautiful.

We headed to the farm in Nebraska to spend Independence Day weekend with my family. The Fourth of July was Deborah's favorite holiday of the year: the fireworks, hanging out with family and friends, watermelon and Bing cherries— she enjoyed the whole package. We tried to find ways to maximize the long weekend.

We left early the morning of the holiday. On the way I came up with a plan not to tell anyone we were engaged. Instead, while we were having lunch, Deborah should try to keep her hand elevated so my mom and sister would see her new beautiful ring.

At the lunch table, when she held up her hand and with the sun coming through the window, her ring really sparkled. No luck. They were as blind as two old squirrels in an acorn warehouse. I looked at Deborah and rolled my eyes as she looked at me like, "Now what?" I had to start dropping hints.

I said, "Boy, Deborah, that ring you have on is sure bright in the sun," or something to that affect. My niece was having lunch with us as well. Later she said she saw the ring but didn't want to say anything. Finally, the scales fell off my mom's and sisters' eyes, and the shrieking started along with the congratulatory hugs. We enjoyed a good laugh.

The next evening we invited my family and a bunch of my best friends from my hometown out for dinner. There Deborah and I officially announced our engagement. It was a fun evening; the ability to share that time with my closest friends and family was special.

We didn't want a big wedding, so we never set an official date. Instead we started to make our wedding plans secretly. We kept everything under wraps. Deborah started looking for a dress and doing other preparatory work for the big day. She spent a number of hours building her bouquet of flowers.

The rest of July and August flew by. I prepared my house for sale, working around multiple showings for interested buyers, and we made trips to the design center to pick out stuff for the new house.

On Thursday, August 28, we headed to Colorado Springs to meet my cousin at his church. We had decided to elope. By 4:30 p.m. that evening, we were officially hitched. We signed all the appropriate forms, and my cousin snapped some pictures for us with the help of his secretary.

Deborah and I were as excited as two tomcats in a mouse pit!

From the church we headed to the Broadmoor hotel for our honeymoon. It was a grand evening. The hotel left a bottle of champagne waiting for us in our room, and then we ate at their five-star restaurant.

It was as if all the hotel staff knew who we were—almost like we were celebrities. Everywhere we went they acted like they knew us personally. We ended up getting lost (with the help of the champagne) on the way back to our room. Not to worry, the staff knew who we were and where we needed to go.

The next morning, we made our way to Yellowstone National Park. It was a long drive but a good one, and on the way we called family to tell them the news. My mom was a little surprised but not totally. My sisters were excited. They loved Deborah and were happy to have her as part of the family.

I always figured if I ever were to get married, I would

prefer to elope. Deborah had married young, a year or so out of high school, and had already had a traditional wedding ceremony. Eloping just seemed right for the two of us.

We spent a couple of days in Yellowstone. It was my first visit, and it was nice. We saw a fox as we entered the park but not much wildlife after that, which was a bit of a bummer. Being so late in the summer and with the water flows receding, the animals must have been hanging out somewhere other than in the tourist areas.

But there was one major problem: the bed in the lodge must have been older than Old Faithful. It was causing me terrible back pain. All the other rooms in the lodge were booked, so the options were limited. The staff tried to help by stacking a bunch of extra blankets on the mattress to make it cushier—no luck. Even ibuprofen didn't really help. Finally, we decided to move on and headed to Jackson Hole early.

Proverbs 24:27 reads: "Finish your outdoor work and get your fields ready; after that build your home." Some commentaries suggest that this is a broad warning for several areas of life, with one being a warning against getting married too young, that a person should have a certain level of stability in their life as well as being prepared emotionally and financially before tying the knot. Sounded pretty good to me!

How many guys can say that on one day in their forty-eighth year of life they became a husband, a father, and a grandfather all at once?

After forty-eight years, and many, many prayers, I married my dream girl.

Both our prayers were answered.

5

GUT PUNCH

"Boxing is real easy. Life is much harder."

—Floyd Mayweather Jr.

Not getting married until one is forty-eight years old means bringing an eighteen-wheeler loaded with baggage into a relationship. This presents numerous challenges. Selfishness and the inability to recognize Deborah's emotional needs are just two of many weaknesses I brought to our marriage. Of course, Deborah had not been married for seventeen years, so she possessed her views on how life should operate as well. Mix together our individual biases and long-term ingrained habits, and you've got a volatile compound called relational nitroglycerin.

Deborah and I continued our counseling sessions and tried to implement the ideas and suggestions Kenna and Rick were giving us. Kenna kept us on track with our workbook, and after our honeymoon we were about midway through it. The book required us to dig into who we were and what might have impacted how we were wired.

By early September it became apparent my house wasn't

going to sell within the ninety-day window we had to close on the new house. Time was short. Finally, we got a low-ball offer. The potential buyers knew our situation and were trying to buy my house for a song while skipping the dance.

In the midst of our housing dilemma, Dainah and Isabela, also known now as Bela, flew to Denver for a Labor Day weekend visit. It was my first get-together with my new twenty-six-year-old stepdaughter and grandbaby.

Deborah and Dainah thought they'd make a quick trip to the store to gather some supplies and leave me alone to take care of Bela. Their idea nearly freaked me out. Never having been a father myself, I possessed no baby skills and was mentally sweating at the thought of watching Bela. I quickly convinced them that it made more sense for Deborah to watch her precious grandbaby while I drove Dainah to the store. Disaster averted!

It was good to finally meet Dainah. She's a high energy go-getter. We grabbed a chance to talk by ourselves a bit. I liked Dainah and felt a good connection with her, but it was short lived. The next day I was off to Nebraska for my aunt's funeral. Life is always about choices. I would have enjoyed more time with Dainah and Bela, but I knew there would be numerous cousins I rarely got an opportunity to see at my aunt's funeral, and the years kept ticking by. I split my time between the two sides of the family.

Once back in Denver the housing problem needed attention. I went back and forth with our builder's representative, trying to get the builder to come down as much as possible on the purchase price of our new house, so we could make it work financially. The builder could not budge, and I could do nothing else. Our real estate agent was doing all she could to make a deal work but with no success.

We were between a rock and a hard place. By late September, we were forced to cancel our contract on the new house and ask for our deposit back. We were at the end of the road as far as being able to sell my house; nothing else could be done.

Deborah was completely devastated. The new house was exactly what she wanted; a ranch with a walkout basement, open space out back, and a kitchen that she loved. Now it was gone. All the planning and time at the design center picking out cabinets, counter tops, carpet, and flooring, selecting the exterior color and brickwork, and living around all the showings for my house, was all for naught. Poof! It was over!

My house would never qualify for an episode of *Lifestyles of the Rich and Famous*, but it was a nice comfortable home. Unfortunately, it was near a busy road, about fifty yards away to be exact. Over the years, I had became desensitized to the traffic noise, plus the county rebuilt the road, which reduced the noise, or so I thought. But Deborah possessed what I would consider supersonic hearing and could hear in detail every car that went by.

One day while we were talking about the whole mess, and with Deborah near tears, she said, "I am going to die in this place." She thought we would never get out of my house for as long as we lived. I felt like a failure, like I let her down big time.

I tried to convince Deborah to be patient, that God had a plan for why all of this was happening. Of course, I had absolutely no clue what that plan might be or what it might even look like. She wasn't buying my positive mental attitude approach to the situation. So much for Dale Carnegie!

On top of all of this, a nationwide financial crisis swept across the country, and the housing market tanked. We had her condo to contend with also. Deborah had moved to Denver at almost the peak of the real estate market, which meant she paid a premium for her condo unit, and now with the economy heading south, the value of her condo took a massive beating—down almost forty percent. We were way upside down on the mortgage. There was no way we could sell it without bringing a ton of cash to closing.

Now we felt the pressure of two mortgage payments and finding an agency to help us market, rent, and manage her condo. Finally, we found a renter, but with the housing market in turmoil we could not generate enough rental income to come close to covering the monthly mortgage payment, HOA dues, and the agency fees. Something was better than nothing, but it made for some tough sledding and a lot of stress.

We arranged for movers to come and move Deborah's stuff to my house. It was a double day of moving as Deborah owned nicer appliances and wanted to switch mine for hers, which was fine with me, but it meant two trips for the movers, a long day, and more of an expense. Our homes were twenty-two miles apart, but thankfully we each lived close to the same major freeway.

Stress was suddenly surrounding us like the Sioux and Cheyenne Indian tribes surrounded Custer at the Battle of the Little Bighorn, and we had only been married a few weeks. In a blink of an eye, the joy and excitement of getting engaged and married were being consumed like grass in a prairie fire.

The second Sunday in October, we went grocery shopping after church. Reverting to my old task-master ways as a single man, I proceeded to zip through the store and rapidly load all the items on our (my) list. Like most women, Deborah was used to taking her time, looking over items, double-checking to make sure no detail was missed. Unbeknownst to me, my commando style of shopping (search, subdue, and escape at lightning quick speed) set Deborah into a very hurt and very angry state.

After gathering our food, we were off to Deborah's condo to pack up a bunch of her smaller stuff to bring back to my house. While I was driving down the freeway, Deborah exploded vehemently. I was stunned and shocked at her reaction, but then I felt terrible at what I had done and my lack of respect for her feelings while shopping. But the manner and incredible intensity in which she reacted seriously scared me. I had never experienced such an explosive reaction of this sort from anyone for any reason, ever!

We arrived at her condo, packed, loaded up the car, and drove back to the house, all while saying very little to each other.

Underlying Problems

The following week, Deborah and I went to counseling. I was so disturbed by the events of the weekend that I probably broke counseling protocol and sent Kenna an e-mail from work Monday. I explained that I did something really bad to upset the apple cart, but that the reaction was so severe that I honestly thought Deborah was suffering from something . . . maybe bipolar. I knew nothing about bipolar disorder, so why I even suggested it, I don't know. I asked Kenna if she could maybe keep this in mind for our session and see if she could uncover something, anything.

Deborah worked that day, so we were to meet at Kenna's office. When I arrived, Deborah's car was in the parking lot, but she was not in the waiting room. She was already in with Kenna. Red flags went up and sirens went off; I thought I was in big time trouble this go-around.

A couple of minutes later, Kenna came out and told me that Deborah had wanted some time with her alone first. Now I was absolutely sure I was in BIG trouble. I had no doubt that Kenna told Deborah I e-mailed her and some suggestions, and now I was going to get filleted like a bass on a cutting board. My anxiety was rising at an exponential rate while waiting in the lobby. I thought I could see a guillotine through the wall.

In the past, on occasion, as a counseling session wound down with Kenna, it felt as though it became a beat-down session on me and my lack of relationship skills. "Why did you say that to Deborah? Why do you feel the way you do? Why do you feel that you say stupid things?"

Often, I left our sessions feeling pretty worthless about myself and very discouraged. I understood I was incredibly adept at being inept, but some of the counseling sessions left me feeling like my cause was hopeless and I was to blame for every one of our problems.

Now I was positive I was going to get really throttled, like when I was a freshman in high school and my classmates and I were required to hold tackling dummies for the seniors in football practice—pain is imminent, and there is nothing you can do to stop it. Tighten the muscles, close your eyes, and wait for the pummeling.

About ten minutes later, Kenna called me in, and I sat down with Deborah on the couch. Kenna announced that Deborah had something to tell me. Oh boy. I held my breath waiting for the guillotine to fall.

Deborah then proceeded to tell me, in between tears, that she suffered from severe depression, the kind that takes you into deep dark places and thoughts of suicide almost daily. She told me she suffered with it most of her adult life. She truly believed that if I knew about her struggles that I would leave her.

What?!

I was stunned! It was the opposite of what I was expecting, and it felt like Hulk Hogan just gut punched me. What she said was even more painful than what I was expecting. I couldn't believe what I was hearing. Here was my beautiful new wife of only six weeks telling me stuff that nobody wants to believe, or hear, about their loved one—ever! How could this spunky and vivacious woman have this going on?

I suspected Deborah had a minor challenge of some sort. There were signs here and there as we dated, like our first fight and other fights along the way. I thought all our battles were part of the normal cycle of getting to know each other and working through the process of adapting to each other's unique personalities.

I was in no way, shape, or form prepared for the intensity of the situation. And intense isn't even an adequate description.

Back at home, Deborah told me about a time during high school when she attempted to hitchhike somewhere around Price, Utah. In those days a guy named Ted Bundy was running around Utah and Colorado kidnapping and murdering women. Whether she knew Ted Bundy by name or just knew there was some very dangerous guy potentially in the area, I am not sure. She told me she thought if she were kidnapped and murdered, it would not be as hard on her parents as if she killed herself.

My head was spinning! All this information within a few of hours was an overload. Circuit breakers were being tripped in my brain. It made me hurt to hear how severe her struggles were. Deborah talked occasionally about her boyfriend from high school and other high school friends. I have seen their pictures and graduation notes in her yearbooks. Would not one of them have known about her struggles? What about her teachers or coaches? Did they have any idea?

Deborah never told anyone about her internal battles— not her parents, her brother, her children, or her best friends, and certainly not me. She really liked Kenna and felt completely comfortable with her, and most importantly she trusted her. Kenna was the first person Deborah trusted enough to tell about her deepest struggles. The time was right for Deborah to tell someone, but it was no easy task for her to do so.

While I was in the waiting room, Kenna told Deborah that she had to tell me. That was a frightful thought for Deborah.

Revealing Moments

I think we all prefer to hide our deepest struggles. That way we don't have to face possible judgment, rejection, and stereotypes. Plus, then we don't have to confront the source of where these struggles come from. Confronting our weaknesses requires going down a very rutted and rocky road with steep embankments on each side.

Through counseling it came out that one of Deborah's biggest fears was being abandoned. Where and how exactly do our deep-seated fears take root? That is tough to determine. "We are in this together," I told her. "And we took an oath before God for better or for worse. Granted things were looking worse, but I made a promise, and I am not going to break that promise no matter what."

We spent the rest of that difficult session discussing bipolar disorder and other mental health challenges that could be playing into Deborah's depression and suicidal thoughts. On top of everything else Deborah began suffering the effects of menopause, which only added more complexity to her mounting health issues. Kenna asked Deborah to promise to call her any time day or night if the suicidal thoughts ever intensified. She asked a lot of probing and tough questions about how the depression and suicidal tendencies manifested. She asked Deborah about when she was feeling suicidal. Did she have a chosen method she would use? The bottom line was that prescription drugs were an issue. I had acquired a number of pain meds over the years from various surgeries. I hadn't been using them, but I'd never thrown them out. It was time to dispose of them and fast! Deborah knew they were in the house. When we got home, I went through all the cabinets, packed up all the bottles of pain meds, and securely disposed of them.

The three of us came to an agreement that Deborah should start seeing a physician, preferably a psychiatrist, to dial in a treatment plan. We quickly found that scheduling an appointment with a psychiatrist was not an easy task as they are in high demand, so we started with our primary care physician. Our first appointment was fairly lengthy, and the doctor thought Deborah exhibited long-term patterns of bipolar disorder based on an extensive list of questions about her past experiences and medical history. He explained that the root of bipolar disorder is an imbalance of energy. That was a new and interesting explanation. People have extreme swings in energy from going at a high pace of work or activity for an extended time followed by low periods of energy. I also didn't realize that depression and bipolar disorder are linked. The doctor's explanation made sense to me and was at a level I could comprehend.

Of course, Deborah always understood doctor talk with her healthcare training as a dental hygienist and through helping her first husband with his medical school studies. I escorted her to a number of doctor's appointments regarding some of her other medical issues, and it usually sounded like Mandarin Chinese when Deborah and a doctor got into a deep discussion. My eyes would glaze over, and at times I would have to ask for a translation.

Our doctor talked about different medications and the treatment plans as well as side effects. So we began a long process to dial in a medication plan that would hopefully be helpful. We would start with a low level dose of one of the newer drugs, build up the dose or add another medication, all the while checking her response.

Deborah was skeptical and worried. She said she tried similar types of pills years before, and they caused some bad side effects that she did not want to experience again. The doctor was pretty sure the newer medications would not cause the same side effects.

My role was to be an observer. I was to look for subtle changes in Deborah from before and after she started a new drug or the dosage was changed. I was to be at all of the physician follow-ups. There was no problem with that from my perspective as we were in this together.

Deborah was a trooper. Once there was a diagnosis, she went online and read all she could about bipolar disorder. She went to a bookstore and bought large books on the subject. She was a voracious reader and could easily read two books to my one, if not more, in short order.

Once she was finished with a book, she wanted me to read it next. Unfortunately, I barely opened any of them. I was swamped with work, and her speed-reading intimidated me. Me the snail and her the hare. I never got to them. I also think I feared reading them for what I would learn about what Deborah was really dealing with.

For most of my life, I had an arrogant attitude about mental illness and was demeaning toward anyone who suffered from it. In hindsight, that was terrible of me considering my grandmother suffered greatly from some form of mental illness, as did others in my family. In the 1930s, my granddad moved his family from the farm in Nebraska to New York City for part of a year so Grandma could go through shock treatments. So much for wanting to go back to the good old days.

A couple of years before I met Deborah, I was having a beer with my buddy Doug. I made a smart-ass remark about Prozac. He then proceeded to tell me he took Prozac; he told me why and how it helped him. Of course, I felt like a complete lowlife. He told me in a kind way when he could have blasted me out of the water for being such an ignoramus. I believe that was the start of God working on my attitude in preparing me to be a helpful husband for Deborah.

Now I was faced with a severe mental illness firsthand with my new wife, and it was very humbling.

In high school, two buddies and I had joined the Nebraska High School Rodeo Association. At our first rodeo, I drew the top bull, which in layman's terms means the biggest, meanest bucking critter in the lot. Once I realized this situation, I went about trying to trade bulls with other cowboys. One of my buddies, whose dad was a world-class bull rider back in the day, informed me that I could not trade bulls. Ernie (such a sweet name for two-thousand pounds of furry) blew me apart in a split second. I lay in the dirt unconscious, and they couldn't even close the bucking shoot gate.

That is how life felt right now. Our marriage was just out of the gate, and we were getting bucked in a violent way.

We continued counseling with Kenna, digging into each of our quirks and behavior patterns. Deborah had been the one to suggest counseling, and I was all in, always up on each chapter of the workbook Kenna suggested. But eventually I started to notice a reluctance on Deborah's part to continue counseling. Soon, she was doing less of the homework.

And to be honest, we started to use Kenna as crutch. We were going to counseling sessions twice a month. Instead of learning to resolve conflicts ourselves, we would wait until we were sitting with Kenna. Eventually, we all agreed this was becoming problematic and that we should cut our sessions back to once a month to force Deborah and me to work through things on our own.

The counseling bills were also starting to add up. With two mortgages and all the other living expenses, we felt we needed to cut back everywhere we could. So, we killed two birds with one stone, so to speak.

The middle chapters in the workbook required us to dig even deeper into our past, and in the back of my mind I began to understand that we were getting into territory that caused Deborah to be especially hesitant. At times you could see it in her face, and other times you could hear it in her voice. I did not press the issue too hard. We were getting too close to something for Deborah, but I had no clue what or how to talk to her about it, and she offered no information.

On Halloween 2008, I flew to Oklahoma City. One of my

cousins and I were going to the Nebraska-Oklahoma football game. It was a good trip, and we spent time tailgating with my former clients and friends, though the game was a mind-boggling beat down. Nebraska and Oklahoma were old rivals with many battles that came down to the end of the game, but that one was over almost as fast as the coin toss.

Deborah was grateful for a weekend alone. Having me away and a quiet house to herself was a break she looked forward to. As much as we loved each other, learning to live with each other was a huge adjustment, so periodic time apart gave us both a bit of breathing room.

After I returned, however, she told me she experienced some very intense emotional struggles during the weekend. The depression and suicidal thoughts hit her hard while I was away. She did not want to call or give any hint that anything was wrong as she thought it might disrupt my weekend, or that I might even decide to fly home. This seriously concerned me, but I really didn't know what I should do, so I did nothing. I just kept it in the back of my mind. As old Forrest Gump would say, "Stupid is as stupid does."

More Health Issues

In early December, Deborah had a hysterectomy. She experienced severe health issues for a number of months relating to this problem. I had gone with her to see the specialist even before we were married. Finally, the only option to get her health back on track was to go under the knife.

Surgery day came. The surgeon came out and told me everything went well. He said Deborah should be fine once fully recovered. That was a bit of good news, considering all the chaos during the first few months of marriage.

I stayed in the hospital overnight with her even though our house was only ten minutes away. In the middle of the night, while heavily medicated, she woke up and felt so bad about me sleeping on a bench that she insisted I get in bed with her so I could be comfortable. She was incredibly cute in her request and insistence. But I assured her that I would be fine. The next morning we had a good laugh when I told her about her request.

Before Deborah's surgery, we had seriously thought of going on a cruise with a family of friends, but the surgery blew that out of the water. Deborah was bummed because it had been a while since her last vacation, and she was really looking forward to the trip. Now she needed to use her few vacation days for surgery and recovery.

Christmas was fast approaching, and we decided in advance to head to the farm for Christmas with my family. We were in need of some time out of town again. In the meantime, Deborah came to the conclusion that her phone was shot, and she needed a new one. She shopped around and found what she wanted: a green slide phone.

Green was Deborah's favorite color. Anything green would be given first consideration regardless of the functionality. Color was primary; function was secondary. It took all my wits to convince her not to buy the dang phone; we were short of cash. "Let's wait until post-Christmas sales hit," I told her. Finally, I was able to convince her not to buy the phone just yet.

There was a lot of December left to get through: office Christmas parties, friends Christmas parties, post-surgery doctor's appointments, and appointments to monitor her bipolar medications. There seemed to be some slight improvement early on, but then there were side effects from the medications that were causing problems for Deborah. That is what she feared the most: the side effects.

Being bipolar was not Deborah's only struggle. By the end of 2007, Deborah complained of physical pain. Twenty-five years as a dental hygienist had exacted a heavy toll on her body. Her back, neck, and shoulders gave her constant problems. We tried chiropractic and massage, but her body was so out of kilter that even those healing efforts left her in residual pain.

After we were married, it was not uncommon for Deborah to take six ibuprofen pills when she would get ready for bed just so she could sleep. She never told me, but she probably needed to take pain relievers during the day as well.

During our sessions with the doctor we discussed the physical pain issue, and eventually he prescribed gabapentin to help manage Deborah's body pain. It definitely helped her sleep better, but again there were side effects that caused other problems. She experienced dizziness, and one day she fell while going up the stairs at home and hurt her elbow.

We were still having regular counseling sessions with Kenna and going through the workbook. But as good as things could be going, we just as quickly could have a dust up. I kept wondering if this was just part of marriage or if the bipolar diagnosis played a part.

On Christmas Day, we opened presents with my family. I had several good gifts for Deborah, but I made sure the phone was the last one she opened. And when she opened that last present, she shrieked with joy. It caught my family by surprise, but eventually everyone laughed and wanted to know what the heck Santa brought Deborah. It was her new green phone. That was a fun day, and one I will never forget.

Over the years I cherished many good Christmas holidays with my family, but I was always alone in a sense. With Deborah at my side, Christmas of 2008 topped them all.

We headed back to Denver with my mom and sisters in tow, as our cousin's daughter was getting married right after Christmas. Once that was behind us and the family left town, Deborah and I settled in for a quiet New Year's Eve. We needed it.

You could say 2008 was the best of times and the worst of times, to paraphrase Charles Dickens.

We were both excited to get married, but the housing situation, Deborah's illnesses, and our interpersonal battles made for a very challenging year. The intensity of it all was at times overwhelming.

Nevertheless, I felt blessed. And, of course, one of my oldest prayers had been answered.

6

YEAR OF CHAOS

"I believe the ability to think is blessed. If you can think about a situation, you can deal with it. The big struggle is to keep your head clear enough to think."

—Richard Pryor

The new year came out of the gate in chaos. On New Year's Eve, I fell asleep watching a movie with Deborah, which caused her to be angry. While she vigorously vented her displeasure, I made an incredibly stupid statement, which only caused her to become angrier, and the argument went down, down, down in a burning ring of fire.

Deborah was a runner. She would run from conflict. As she once told me: "I can run, and I always do." But I wasn't too good with conflict either. Over the past few years I came to realize that I tended to avoid conflict by shutting down emotionally or mentally, and sometimes physically.

That is what I did New Year's Day. I checked out physically. Our fight erupted right as the Nebraska Cornhuskers Gator Bowl game was starting and that just added to the household turmoil. New Year's Day is a day for family, food, football, and lying around being slothful, and that was my plan. The plan was not going as planned.

In a fit of frustration and stupidity I left the house; I just drove off. I headed to a park to listen to the game on the radio and tried to calm my rattled nerves. But that didn't work, so I headed to Old Chicago's. I was pretty sure there wouldn't be any Husker fans there as it was not one of the "official watch sites" of the Coloradoans for Nebraska club. I could just watch the game alone and not be bothered by anyone. Plus, I was now in a foul mood and no one would want to talk to me for very long anyway. Several hours later, I headed home.

We were a runner and an avoider having a five-alarm fight. It's tough to get much resolved in that dynamic. But we had to keep trying as we were joined at the hip now. So plow forward we did.

As I mentioned earlier, the house we put a deposit on back in June of 2008 fell through. We couldn't sell my house and had to give up Deborah's dream house. Deborah was crushed. I told her God had a plan and that's why the new house didn't work out. Be patient, I told her; surely something would change. She had no reason to believe a word I said.

In January I talked with our real estate agent, and she thought we should list my house again in March. She said March was one of the best times of the year to list a house and thought we would have a much better chance to sell it than we did the previous summer. So, the start of 2009 was loaded with another round of stress as we prepared Deborah's condo to rent and my house for sale, for the second time.

Ever since Deborah moved into my house she had to drive forty miles one way to her office in Arvada. It was just one more source of stress for her. She didn't like driving in general but add in some traffic and then mix in some bad weather and it was a recipe for high anxiety.

One morning I called her while she was on the freeway in a blizzard. She was so on edge that she was screaming and crying at me at the same time. The girl was a mess, and I needed to do something sooner rather than later to help her. On her next day off I took her car to the tire shop and bought her a set of studded mud and snow tires.

That one little strategic change with her car made a massive difference in her daily commute. Those studded snow tires gave her more control of her car and a boost of confidence. I was a hero in her eyes. She kept those studded tires on her car until the last legal day in April and made sure they were back on the car the first legal day in the fall. They were like a security blanket for her.

Knowing the stress she was under driving up to her job, I started calling dental offices closer to home that specialized in periodontics to see if there were openings. Deborah had started to specialize in periodontal dental hygiene before we were married and really enjoyed the challenge of the work. Unfortunately, with the economy in the tank, very few offices were hiring. But a number of them took our information just in case.

Everywhere we turned there was stress. When we needed a smooth path, it was time for one of our road trips. For whatever reason, leaving the house and getting out of town on a road trip soothed the trouble between us. These road trips were therapeutic. Of course, our honeymoon to Yellowstone and Jackson Hole had been the best road trip.

That January we started to brainstorm where we should head to next, knowing we desperately needed a getaway. I think we could both feel a storm approaching over the horizon and knew we needed to be proactive. The sooner we could load up and head out the better.

We wanted to go somewhere we hadn't been before and that was within a manageable driving distance. We chose Taos, New Mexico. We picked the first weekend of February, and after some Internet searches we booked a room at a bed-and-breakfast.

We were both anticipating getting on the road. Taos was about three hundred miles from our house in Parker, Colorado, and we made the drive in good time. We spent a couple of hours in the old town area shopping and checking out various stores and galleries.

Taos was smaller than we expected, and it didn't take long for us to cover the major tourist spots. Then we spent some time driving around town. We found our bed-and-breakfast, and as we were unpacking Deborah dropped a few items out of her pack, one of which was a tube of lip balm that proceeded to roll completely across our room's wood floor at a nice clip. We both looked at each other in stunned amazement that our room could be off-kilter that much. It should have been a warning.

We found a nice place to have dinner, and once back at the room we broke out the cards and played a few hands of gin rummy. Deborah and I enjoyed playing cards together and somewhere along the line we also started playing dominos. Our card playing and dominos helped keep the two of us grounded from all the stuff that could get between us during the day.

There was no set agenda for Saturday so we jumped into bed Friday evening knowing that we could sleep in a bit. When I woke up the next morning something didn't feel right. I was itching all over. When I told Deb about the itching, she said my back was covered with little red marks. Then she realized she had her share as well, and her head was itching. Evidently, our bed was full of bedbugs or some other small nefarious creature that snacked on us while we sawed logs.

After breakfast and a few scratching sessions, we headed out to explore more of Taos. We stopped in some art galleries we had no business being in as the prices of most pieces could buy a good tractor back home. The salespeople sucked us into the vortex of the world of high-priced art and nearly had us convinced we should buy something. Somehow we escaped unscathed.

Then on a whim we decided to drive down to Santa Fe. It was less than a two-hour drive, and again driving was good for us. Maybe we should have considered buying an eighteen-wheeler and become over-the-road truckers.

Eventually we ended up in one of the oldest—if not the oldest—hotel in the tourist district of Santa Fe for a drink. It was a cool place and a thought hit us: how much were the rooms here? To our luck they had a discounted room rate for some reason. It wasn't much more than the Bedbug Inn, and it appeared very clean, which sold us. We booked a room.

We quickly hoofed it to the truck and drove back to Taos, loaded up our luggage, told the front desk we had to leave town, and got a refund for our second night. Then we drove back to Santa Fe. The extra drive was worth it. We enjoyed the evening in Santa Fe, hung around Sunday morning, then headed back to Denver.

In the midst of all of our hectic busyness, Deborah's big birthday was fast approaching. She was having a real struggle with the idea of turning fifty. I kept trying to make plans though she was reluctant to celebrate her birthday. She just wanted to go to work, not tell anyone, and then come home, as if not celebrating would make it *not* happen. Sensing that this was more difficult for her than I could comprehend, I penned a little poem for her which I gave to her with some flowers:

Life's journey takes us down a path
we can't control
Otherwise known as God's great gift of time
All too often, though, it leaves us
feeling less than whole
But with our eyes fixed on God's prize,
we'll be just fine

Even then, as time whisks by,
we find it oh so hard to focus
But just remember, the Grace of God abounds
And when the rigors of life
feel like a swarm of locusts
Never forget God's love, and mine too,
and that we are both around

Joshy

Back to Reality

We were ready to list the house again by late March, so we mentally prepared for dealing with multiple showings each week, and sometimes each day. After a long day of work, we might have to go out to dinner and find some place to whittle away our time while waiting for the prospective buyers to depart. It is the weary part of selling a home.

Fast approaching was April 3, 2009, granddaughter Bela's first birthday. Deborah and I flew to Indianapolis to be on hand for the festivities. Deborah loved her granddaughter and looked forward to every opportunity to be with her. It was one of the craziest kid birthdays I ever witnessed, not that I have witnessed many.

Bela was the first grandbaby on her dad's side of the family, and most all of the family lived within driving distance of Indy. Grandparents, great-grandparents, aunts and uncles, great-aunts and great-uncles, cousins, family friends, and who knows who else were all on hand. The gifts nearly filled the living room. The ritual of opening the gifts took the better part of the afternoon and left all of us exhausted. It was truly a birthday present spectacle.

At one point in the afternoon, Deborah started to struggle with the crowdedness in the house during the festivities. It was just too many people crammed all together for her. I did my best to calm her, but until everyone cleared out and headed home, her stress and anxiety levels were climbing the charts.

That Sunday morning, we headed to church, ate a quick lunch, and then it was off to the airport. Even though it was a quick trip, we had a lot of fun overall, and Deborah got to spend time with her precious granddaughter. It was also good to get out of our hometown for a few days again.

The next Sunday was Easter Sunday. It was a rainy day. As we were lounging around the house, out of the blue, Deborah got some shocking news; her boss in Arvada sent her a text message saying he was letting her go. Of course, this was a completely gutless way of firing someone, especially on a Sunday and Easter Sunday at that. Deborah had no warning and was totally devastated. I wasn't as concerned. Her dental job was way up in north Denver and a long drive each day through the dreaded traffic. In fact, I felt a bit of relief for both of us.

I tried to reassure her that we would be okay without the Arvada job. I told her she would find a new full-time job. Of course, she felt she needed to contribute her fair share to the household and all, but I knew that the long commute combined with the long workdays were really taking a toll on her health. And with her health suffering as it was, she would be better off without the multiple layers of stress that came with the job. Nevertheless she struggled with the situation and harbored a lot of anger for her ex-boss.

Early May was busy with two road trips. First, we made a run to the farm in Nebraska. Then the following weekend we were on the road to Salt Lake City to see Deborah's best friend and her aunt. We loaded up her son Mike to bring him back to Denver. We made a run down to Price to see Deborah's mom, Ina, and then back to Denver. Before we left for Salt Lake City, we had another big flare up. It took almost the whole drive to Salt Lake City for us to loosen up.

Deborah was picking up some consistent part-time dental

hygiene work through a placement agency. At one of the clinics she quickly made friends, as usual. One such friend asked Deborah if she would be interested in joining a quilting group. Deborah was excited and all-in. The group met once a month and Deborah made new friends. Having girlfriends was important for Deborah.

Memorial Day weekend meant another trip to the farm as it was my thirtieth class reunion. Deborah was able to meet a lot of my high school classmates and friends. My graduation class was only twenty-four students, and we were a pretty close group. Deborah didn't especially enjoy these types of events, but she did well, and we enjoyed ourselves.

Later that summer, we headed to the farm again, this time for the big Nordhausen Family Reunion. My maternal grand-mother was a Nordhausen from Germany and moved to America in the 1920s. Grandma had eleven brothers and sisters. Most of them came to the United States and ended up in Nebraska. The tri-annual Nordhausen Family Reunion usually draws about three hundred family members—cousins stacked on top of cousins. I was really excited to have Deborah along for the big shindig.

Before we left for my class reunion, we found a renter for Deborah's condo, and an offer arrived for my house. We started looking at new homes again; in fact, we went back out to where our first house was located. We really liked the area and the builder. Then a miracle happened. The last lot for a walkout basement that would accommodate the ranch model we wanted was available. In fact, they had already started on the house as a spec home. We quickly signed the papers and wrote a check for the deposit.

As it worked out, with the real estate market crashing, we were able to get a way better deal on the second house (same model) and with a lower interest rate. I reminded Deborah that God did have a plan for us, and it worked out better for us with the nine-month wait. She was super excited that we were back on track for her new dream home and would be moving out of my house.

Now came a dilemma and more tumult; my house was going to close in early July, but our new house would not be ready until the end of August. We had a very limited amount of time to find some place to live for only two and a half months, knowing that no landlord is interested in a three-month lease.

We found a couple online who needed to move out of their condo almost at the same time we needed to be out of my house. Not only that, they only had three months left on their lease, which would end just after our new house was to be completed. As long as our house stayed on schedule, it was going to work out perfectly. They also had a washer and dryer they wanted to sell us. I told Deborah I would not pay more than $250 for the set. We asked them their price: $250. Everything was perfect. We knew God's hand was involved and that He was answering the prayers of two nervous couples.

Now we hired the movers again and moved all of our stuff from my house to the condo and a couple of garages at the complex; we could not fit everything into the condo, but thankfully there were extra garages to rent.

None of this was easy doing. Deborah's son, Mike, had come to live with us for the summer before he went off to college, so he got caught up in the excitement and frenzy. Adding to the craziness, Deborah felt like she was on fire most of the time. I'm not sure if the bipolar meds caused it or menopause or both, but she was very uncomfortable and set the AC to deep freeze. I could barely stand it and wore a sweatshirt while she baked like a potato. Needless to say, all of this caused a couple of ugly blowups while at the condo. I felt bad for Mike for having to be in the middle of our struggles while we were all cooped up in such a small living space.

Deborah and I went out to the new house often to see how it was coming along. We couldn't wait to move in. When the week finally came to move, we hired movers for a third time within a year. Three major moves in the span of twelve months! We were exhausted but managed to survive even with our fights.

Deborah was still making regular visits to our physician to try to get her medications dialed in. At that point, I could honestly say I was not seeing any noticeable improvement from the drugs. Deborah still seemed to be battling some-thing, and I wasn't sure I understood what she was battling or that it was even bipolar disorder. The other issue was that the drugs were starting to have side effects that were causing other problems. It was like a Catch-22, the exact concern she voiced when we started the medication plan.

As the bad relationship days increased, I became increas-ingly frustrated. I had a minor issue for which I scheduled a visit with our doctor, but it was an excuse. I really wanted to talk to him about Deborah. I told him I was not seeing much improvement in Deborah with the bipolar drugs and wondered if we were on the right track because the tension between us appeared to be escalating and was becoming very tiring. He told me to hang in there and be patient. Perhaps it would take a while to find the right combination and doses of medications to help Deborah.

I loved Deborah dearly and wanted to do all I could to help her. But being a fallible human being, I would get flus-tered and develop a bad attitude. I was not always the good husband she needed. I did, however, listen to our doctor and agreed to give the medications more time.

Dream Home

On August 22, 2009, we officially made the move into Debo-rah's dream home. Mike was there to help with the small stuff, but again we hired a moving company to move the big stuff.

We racked up a pretty big bill for the year just for moving expenses.

The following weekend was our first anniversary, so we scheduled a weekend away. It was a good getaway, and one we needed after the chaos of the summer. A few weeks later, Dainah and grandbaby Bela came for a visit. Deborah was elated, but a day before Dainah and Bela arrived we had a severe dust up. I can't even remember what we argued about. I just know the tension was high in the house when they showed up.

We took them to the zoo and introduced Bela to giraffes. She was mesmerized and continues to have a fascination with giraffes.

Our blowups continued for weeks after that visit, leading to a nine-alarm fight. Deborah's anger toward me was off the charts, so much so that I was truly frightened. It was a bad one. Her anger was different this time; it was more intense and relentless. In fact, it lasted a number of days. I was truly scared for her safety. I wondered if the suicidal inclinations might be at play.

Listen, I'm a farm boy, and my college major was agricultural economics not psychology or medicine. I had limited skills or knowledge for what to do in mental health situations. Yet, I knew I had to do something, so I called Dainah for help.

I told Dainah that I was really scared for her mom. We decided that Deborah's mom should know what was happening. Dainah called her grandmother and gave her a rundown of the situation. Deborah had already informed her mom and the kids of her bipolar diagnosis.

Next, I met with Kenna and Rick together to ask for their advice and feedback. I also met with our Bible study teacher and contacted a psychologist friend. I was looking for help from anyone to figure out what might be happening with Deborah. I was in a desperate search to find some way to help her.

Though Deborah calmed down a week later, it was a nerve-rattling experience for me and remained in the back of my mind. All the fights, her anger, just couldn't be normal.

Christmas in the New Home

It had been a while since Deborah celebrated Christmas with both her kids. So, we planned to have them all to our house for Christmas: her son, daughter, son-in-law, and, of course, Bela. Deborah was super excited, and so was I.

But we had another fight, for whatever reason, in late December. This time my anger towards Deborah was intense. We were scheduled to go to the farm to have a pre-Christmas celebration with my family, but Deborah called my mom to tell her she could not make the trip and that set me off. I was stewing like a teapot the whole drive to the farm and for most of the weekend.

This was the first time I became truly angry with Deborah. It was an intense type of anger and unhealthy.

Anger is a difficult emotion. For years I dealt with anger, or hatred, toward people—my high school principal, guys from college, whoever crossed me—and all for very stupid and selfish reasons. Anger can consume you and control your life. Somehow you have to make sure to not let it slip into your soul.

One Sunday when living in Sacramento years earlier, while I sat in church, the pastor said something that rattled my soul. I can't remember exactly what he said, but it made me realize what a hypocrite I'd been, and years of pent-up anger was released. Rarely did I get so angry anymore. That fight with Deborah triggered old emotions. When the anger subsided, I felt terrible and told Deborah about it and told her I was sorry. We finally sat down the night before her kids arrived. We agreed we needed to put the argument aside and focus on having a great Christmas with her family. We decided we would have a discussion when they left.

Dainah, Jason, and Bela arrived first. Then Mike flew into Denver. As they were flying in, a major snowstorm hit. The roads were still open, though, and everyone made it to our house in fine shape.

We spent the first couple of days running around seeing exhibits at the Denver Museum of Natural History, shopping, and going to movies. After the church Christmas program, we all hunkered down at the house for the next couple of days, exchanging gifts, cooking meals, playing games, and being generally lazy. The five days that Dainah, Jason, Bela, and Mike were with us were a grand time. It was a wonderful Christmas, and Deborah thoroughly enjoyed it. We were sad to see her family leave.

Being single my whole life, I almost never missed going home to Nebraska for Christmas to be with my family, but it did not matter this year. Christmas with Deborah's family was perfect. I love the holiday season, and that was a Christmas I will never forget. I felt like Clark Griswold at the very end of the movie *National Lampoon's Christmas Vacation* where he says, "I did it." Well, I finally did it. I celebrated Christmas with my new family, and it was worth the wait.

It had been a year of chaos mixed with blessings and more answered prayers.

7

THE FURY OF ILLNESS

Melissa: "Is there such a thing as an F5?
What would that be like?"
Dusty: "The finger of God."

—The movie *Twister*

About a week before Christmas 2009, I caught the flu, but with the help of my chiropractor and some homeopathic formulas I was able to kick the bug pretty quickly. Unfortunately, I think Deborah picked up the bug from me. She started complaining of not feeling well shortly after Dainah and her family left town. The flu smacked her hard, and along with menopause and bipolar, she was just not in a good mood much of the time.

For New Year's Eve, Deborah and I went out for dinner and then came home to play cards and watch a movie.

To start 2010 off on a good note, Deborah wanted to go through the book *The Love Dare* together. It was a well-known relationship book at the time made in conjunction with the movie *Fireproof*, and I was all for it. After only a couple of chapters Deborah became upset and threw her book away, which left me puzzled. I wasn't sure if the bipolar was causing more intense problems, or if it was due to the flu bug, but it seemed she was angry with me more often. I knew I could be a numbskull sometimes, but I didn't think I was that bad. Not only that, but she wasn't getting any better from the flu; in fact, she was getting sicker.

Deborah brought up the topic of divorce a couple of times in the past when there was elevated stress in our relationship. Now she brought it up again. Her opinion was that if two people could not get along any better than we did at times, maybe being apart was better than together. My opinion was that we made a promise to God and each other. For better or for worse we were one, and we should make the effort to work through our struggles.

Deborah decided that we should set a goal to meet certain benchmarks through the year, and if we did not see improvement by year-end, we should consider legal separation as of January 2011. So we sat down and wrote out an agreement; we detailed what the benchmarks should be to improve our relationship. Some were her ideas, and some were mine. We agreed on the following:

1. Weekly "check-ins" each Sunday to see how we are feeling about each other.
2. Physical contact every day.
3. Sleeping in the same bed every night.
4. Not dredging up old hurts.
5. Forgiving each other.
6. Praying daily together.
7. Rings stay on, no matter what.
8. If there is an issue, don't go to bed angry.
9. If you love me, then say it.

We were on our own here, which in some ways was good. After Deborah lost her job, we stopped seeing Kenna. Cash flow was tight, and I could sense a reluctance with Deborah as we delved into the later chapters of the relationship study book we were working through. There was much I did not understand or know about, and I did not want to push her emotionally when she resisted.

In January, Deborah told me she wanted to start weaning herself off of the bipolar medication. I knew the meds were causing side effects that were creating other problems for her, so I supported her decision. Quite frankly, by this time I didn't think the meds were helping her anyway, and I was beginning to wonder if she was even bipolar. I was sure she suffered from something, but I had no clue what it could be.

I kept seeing Rick on occasion to try to figure out what I was doing to cause problems or to try to figure out what Deborah might be dealing with. Rick advised me to read a book by a psychiatrist who was bipolar. After reading the book I was convinced Deborah was not bipolar. She didn't exhibit many of the classic signs of bipolar disorder, which explained the ineffectiveness of the medications.

Rick also recommended a book on borderline personality disorder. It was eye-opening to learn about all the extremely difficult mental health challenges so many people are afflicted with. It was a humbling read. But again, the symptoms were not what I saw in Deborah.

After those two books Rick recommended a third book called *Emotional Vampires*. The title is more ominous than the book. All these books I kept at the office and did my studying during the workday.

In late January, I broke a crown on a back tooth and got a nasty infection. I needed a root canal. That evening, I zonked out in my recliner while Deborah went to the quilt shop. A few hours later Deborah came home. She sat down in her recliner next to mine. Her first words were, "Well, there was a PetSmart next to the quilt shop." I knew immediately where this was going. Deborah loved animals, but dogs were at the top of her animal totem pole. I was pretty sure she fell in love with a dog.

Growing up on the farm I had several dogs. They were my everyday buddies because most of my school friends lived so far away. We lived way out in the middle of nowhere, and a good bit of my time was spent running the pastures, fields, and river bottoms with my border collie, Laddy.

My dad got Laddy as a pup within a year after I was born, so we were almost the same age, and we grew up together. He was a great dog.

However, all my dogs while I was growing up were outdoor dogs. (Mother's rules for good housekeeping.) They had their doghouse or the barn to sleep in and hunted for a lot of their own food or got table scraps and sometimes even a big bowl of fresh milk from the cow. I just never felt good about having a dog cooped up in a house after growing up with dogs that ran free out on the farm.

Deborah and Mike were forced to give up their dog when they moved into her condo in Littleton; either the HOA rules required it or a neighbor was causing a fuss. She thought she might never have a dog again. Of course, she had the cookie dog jar I gave her for Christmas, but that really didn't count.

"They have a really cute schnauzer."

My suspicions were confirmed. "And you want him?" I asked.

"Well," she said, "will you just go look at him?"

"You want to adopt him, don't you?"

"Will you just go look at him with me?" she insisted.

I enjoyed the fun exchange. I knew she found the puppy she wanted, so we loaded up at about eight that evening and drove back out to the pet store. They brought the little guy into an interview room. He was a miniature German schnauzer who was scared out of his wits. He hid in the corner and would barely come over to me. I had to crouch down on the floor to pet him and relieve his fear. They thought he was about three years old and must have suffered some abuse.

I told Deborah if this was the dog she wanted, then we would get him. Deborah was very intuitive. Evidently, she connected with the dog the minute she looked into his eyes. We had made the rounds at pet stores before to look at the dogs, but never once did she see one she had to have —until now.

We signed all the papers and paid the fees that night. We needed to wait until the next day to pick him up as we had to clear a twenty-four-hour adoption screening process. I was almost a real parent of a house dog!

Since he was a German dog, and my family is mostly German, I had a name picked out for him from the get-go: Otto. Deborah liked the name as well. Upon entering the house, Otto ran down the hall and peed on a doorjamb. I told Deborah she'd have to house-train him quickly because I had no clue what to do except holler "stop!"

While we were at the store picking up Otto, we bought a ton of stuff: bed, bowls, dog food, and various treats. I followed Deborah's lead on everything. She was the expert. She bought a box of treats called Greenies and immediately gave one to Otto. Later that afternoon she gave Otto another Greenie. He sure liked those treats.

Bedtime came, and we put Otto's new bed in our bedroom on Deborah's side. We got him settled in, and then we jumped into bed. It wasn't long before we heard Otto's collar tinkling; he was out of bed snooping around. We turned the light on, got up, and settled him back into his bed. A few minutes later he was up again, and so were we. As good dog parents we tried to explain to him that it was bedtime and he needed to stay in bed, believing he understood what we were saying. Sure!

For a third time Otto was up. Arrg! I got up first, without turning on the light, and for whatever reason went into the bathroom in the dark. Deborah got up, too, and then from the bathroom I heard her scream, "Son of a b———!"

Of course, the room was dark, but instinctively I knew what happened. I hesitated to turn on the light because I was trying not to laugh (and that would have been a terrible, terrible mistake for which I would likely not have survived the night). I quickly gathered myself. "What happened?" I asked, choking back a chuckle.

Otto kept getting up because he needed to take an intense poo, most likely because of the two treats and excitement of a new home. Being in new surroundings, he was getting out of bed to try to find the right place to do his business. Unfortunately, he did so right where Deborah stepped, and she had a foot full of dog poo and was not happy. Looking back it was a memorable first day with our new dog-child.

Otto was the kind of dog that developed a good stink. He required a bath about every two weeks. Early on these baths were a real struggle, and Deborah would bathe him in the bathtub in our spare bathroom. One Saturday, trying to be the helpful husband, I offered to bathe Otto for Deborah and decided I would do so in the big sink in the washroom.

Of course, Otto was in no mood for a bath and the battle was on. All of a sudden, he started yelping in a high pitch and reached up and chomped on my finger that was close to his head. My finger promptly started to bleed. I hollered for Deborah and lifted him out of the sink as he kept yelping.

After I set him down, he pulled himself across the floor, dragging his left rear leg and foot. It looked like his back leg was broken. I was freaking out, and Deborah was screaming at me. It's easy to say what you would do in an emergency, as though you would be Cool Hand Luke. Right? I tended to freeze or panic in emergency situations. One day in college I lost my brakes as I came up to an intersection on campus. Students started pouring across the street. Thankfully, I did not run anyone over. I should have pulled the emergency brake, but I freaked out. And I freaked out now and wasn't thinking straight when the dog looked hurt.

Deborah ran out of the washroom to get her purse and glasses. My brain was somewhere other than where it should have been, and I didn't bother looking for it, or for Deborah. I immediately wrapped Otto in a towel, climbed in the truck, backed out of the garage, and headed down the street. Not only was my brain not present, but I also forgot *my* glasses and my wallet . . . and Deborah!

As I drove down the street, I just happened to look in the rearview mirror and saw Deborah run out of the garage—which I forgot to close. She stopped in the middle of the street with her hands in the air as if saying, "You idiot! Where are you going without me?"

Even at a distance I could see the dumbfounded look on her face. Oops! I stopped, backed all the way down the street, and stopped so she could get in while I retrieved my wallet and glasses. She grabbed Otto and held him as we headed to the vet ER.

Surprisingly, Otto was much calmer on the drive than I was. We got him checked in at the animal hospital, and they sent Otto back to see a doctor. I could see the next morning headlines: "Man breaks dog's leg. Held on felony animal abuse charges at local jail."

A short time later the doctor came out and said he could not find any fractures and it was probably a soft tissue injury. The doctor said Otto seemed fine. However, my checking account and my pride did not feel fine.

We soon learned that Otto was a good actor with a flair for the dramatic—a possible future Oscar nominee. Maybe it was from past abuse, but he tended to overreact. Oh well, he was still our buddy.

Animals are supposed to be relaxing and calming, and I thought with the bipolar—or whatever it was—Otto would be helpful for Deborah. And he was. Otto became Deborah's little buddy. They went everywhere together. Whether I was driving or Deborah was driving, Otto was on her lap. At home, he sat with her in her recliner, and if she could make it work, Deborah would sneak Otto into bed with her. They were two peas in a pod.

Me? Otto didn't pay a lot of attention to me unless I was feeding him or taking him for a walk. Deborah was the cat's meow for him, or the dog's yelp.

Otto could do no wrong in her mind.

Shortly after Deborah and I were married, I developed a snoring habit. It's a mystery how this came about so suddenly. Deborah learned to nudge me while I was sleeping to get me to roll onto my side, which evidently quieted me down.

One night as I was lying wide awake and Otto was over in his bed, I heard some loud snoring. Otto was sawing logs big time. Out of the blue, Deborah throws an elbow into my ribs and said, "Dang it, Josh! Stop snoring." I vociferously defended myself and explained it was her canine buddy who was responsible. She chuckled, but my ribs still hurt.

A few months later I would come to understand what a true blessing from God that Otto was.

Frustrating Search for a Diagnosis

It was now February, and Deborah could still not shake the flu bug, which was turning into a bad case of bronchitis. She saw our primary care doctor who gave her some medications as well as a steroid. Deborah was leery of steroids. She had been on them many times for asthma and bouts of sinusitis, and she was well aware of their negative side effects.

Next, he referred Deborah to an asthma and allergy specialist. She suffered from asthma most of her life and our doctor wondered if maybe some allergy kicked in as well. The specialist then put her on another round of steroids. After this it was off to a rheumatologist for more tests, which also meant more steroids. Fortunately, the tests from the rheumatologist were negative. Deborah was distressed. She worried that she might be developing the same medical issues her dad had suffered from. Deborah had been very close to her dad, and it had been difficult for her to watch his health slowly deteriorate. She talked about this a number of times in the past and was bringing it up again now. She was really scared of going through the same pain and suffering her dad had.

Through all of this, she was also getting very upset with the steroids each doctor prescribed; she endured round after round of steroids. One evening she sat crying and said, "I can't do all these steroids! I keep telling the doctors, and no one will listen." Of course, I did not have her level of medical knowledge and didn't comprehend the severity of what she was saying regarding the steroids.

One of the doctors thought Deborah's issues were because she was allergic to Otto. Her illness did seem to have really ramped up after we brought him home from the store. This was completely devastating news to both of us, but we made the tough decision for Deborah's well-being. We decided to return Otto to the rescue shelter, which was located in the pet store.

The night we took him back was difficult. The little guy was scared out of his wits and shaking uncontrollably. Both of us were near tears when we left the store. We had Otto for only two weeks, and we were already very attached to him. He was truly a special dog, and now he was gone almost as quickly as we adopted him. It was a rough trip to the pet store and then back home. I felt terrible for the guy.

The next afternoon Deborah met with the allergist to review some test results. Holy smokes! Otto was not the problem! Deborah did not have any dog allergies at all. She called me immediately from the doctor's office. Panic set in for both of us. We had to get Otto back before somebody else nabbed the little guy. Each minute was critical!

I dropped everything at the office and started making calls. We got ahold of the store where they had Otto plus the rescue agency and told them the story. "Don't sell him to anyone else! We'll be over as soon as possible to get him!"

Deborah and I met at home and made the mad dash to go get our buddy back. It was a wild two days—from the lowest of lows to exhilaration and excitement in less than forty-eight hours.

Otto was back at home with us where he belonged. All was good with the world for the moment.

Deborah's illness continued. She could not shake whatever she had. Not one of the doctors could diagnose the problem. The only answer we got from the different doctors was to try another round of steroids and then see what happens. This left Deborah exasperated and in a fragile mental state. There seemed to be nothing I could do to help. Why couldn't anyone give us some sound feedback? It was a frustrating situation with no answers in sight.

On May 20, we celebrated my mom's eightieth birthday. She wanted to go to Omaha and enjoy the botanical gardens and zoo, and she wanted to visit my aunt who lived in Council Bluffs, Iowa. A week before heading to Omaha, two of my sisters were in Denver, and we all headed out for dinner. I was always messing with my wedding ring as it was the first time I ever wore a ring. Growing up on the farm we never wore rings because if the ring would get caught on a piece of equipment, you'd lose a finger. After dinner I headed to the men's room and after washing my hands and heading toward the door I flung the paper towel at the wastebasket and heard a ping, which was kind of weird. The next morning, I could not find my wedding ring. I was stumped.

Deborah and I drove from Denver to meet my mom and sisters in Omaha. Deborah and I did our own exploring walking around different parts of Old Town Omaha, but the walks were a struggle for her. The flu and her asthma made for a very slow and labored pace.

We enjoyed the time in Omaha. We took a riverboat cruise for Mom's birthday and were able to hang out with my aunt and cousin, who escorted us around town and hosted a barbeque for us. The house was busy and crowded, which was not a good dynamic for Deborah. With her not feeling well from the flu, it was not long before she needed to leave. So, we headed back to the hotel.

Deborah scheduled another doctor's appointment when we returned home, and this time she was diagnosed with pneumonia. She traveled on a long road trip to Omaha with pneumonia, and we didn't even know it! Who knows how long she suffered from pneumonia. I couldn't believe it. Both of us were frustrated with this news.

Deborah was in tough shape. Besides all the body pains from her dental hygiene work, her sinusitis, asthma, supposed bipolar, and the flu, now she also had pneumonia! Add to the mix the beginning of menopause and throw in the flurry of the successive rounds of steroids, and it's no wonder she was not feeling well and was frequently crabby. I would be, too! Sometimes I wondered how she could even get out of bed, let alone go to work, but she did.

Her work hours picked up as she found a couple more part-time jobs. She liked the crew at one office that was kind of close to home, so those were good workdays for her with limited stress. But still she was working extra hours while dealing with some pretty serious health problems.

Deborah began having problems sleeping and started sleeping in the front bedroom almost every night. This was not uncommon when she was mad at me, but now she did it so as not to wake me. During the evenings she would be coughing and hacking, and the steroids caused her to be wound tighter than a coiled rattler. She would lie in bed reading or watching movies on her laptop until she finally fell asleep from exhaustion in the middle of the night. I honestly do not know how she made it through the days.

One morning she told me the asthma kicked in so hard she needed to use her EpiPen because she couldn't breathe. This was the first time I remembered her using an EpiPen. The EpiPen concept was new to me and sounded ghastly. It made me think of the gross scene in the even grosser movie *Pulp Fiction*. How someone could willingly jab a massive needle into their own body was beyond my comprehension. It gave me the willies!

I did come to understand that it is a serious issue when someone needs an EpiPen. Still the thought of it made me cringe.

My head was spinning like a gyroscope. I was really starting to intensely worry about Deborah's health. I had never been this close to someone going through so many health issues, and I didn't know what to do or say. I tried to be helpful and supportive, but at times I felt helpless. I felt as though I was an irritant for Deborah and only making matters worse.

It was as if she were a walking, talking F-5 tornado of illness.

Even though she was sleeping in the front bedroom, she still wanted a goodbye kiss before I left for the office. I assured her that she would get her goodbye kisses even if she were sound asleep. I would finish breakfast, get dressed for work, and, without my shoes on, I would slowly and quietly make my way down the hall. By summer, her health was so bad that as I went down the hall to give her a goodbye kiss, I had severe feelings of anxiety and fear. I was afraid one morning I would find her dead. I'd pause, take a breath, and ease open the bedroom door. Then I'd look at her lying in bed and try to see if she was breathing. Hesitantly, I would creep over to her. Once I could see that she was indeed breathing, I'd give her a kiss. Sometimes she would mumble, and sometimes she was completely zonked out from her rough night. Then I would quietly leave the house for the office.

During a phone call with Dainah, I told her about my fear of finding her mother dead some morning, but she just thought I was being dramatic and didn't take me seriously. Well, I was serious, extremely serious, and if Dainah would not believe me, who would?

All I could do was pray for my wife. Night after night I prayed, petitioned, and begged God to help Deborah, and yet each day her struggle intensified.

One night during the first week of August, I went to bed at 9:30 p.m. as usual. Deborah stayed up to watch movies and then went to the front bedroom to read and hopefully fall asleep. In the middle of the night, she woke me up in a little bit of a panic. She told me she thought she was having a heart attack.

What?!

I told her we needed to get dressed and head to the emergency room. She said no. I kept insisting we needed to go to the ER, but she wouldn't go. Finally, she asked me if she could get in bed with me. Of course, I said yes, and she crawled in. It was the first time in a long time I wrapped my arms around her, and we fell asleep together.

8

THE DECISION

"Well, there are some things a man just can't run away from."

—John Wayne, *Stagecoach*

The year 2010 was turning into an unbelievably challenging year for both of us. Deborah was ill and only getting sicker, and none of the doctors could give any clear answers as to what she was suffering from let alone provide guidance for healing. Our relationship was more challenging than ever. Though we enjoyed some extremely good times, the bad times were becoming more frequent and more intense. We kept fighting, and Deborah's outbursts were becoming more intense and lasting longer than before. It was as if Deborah were a Molotov cocktail, and I was the spark that set off the explosions. I wondered how she could get so intensely angry, and she would ask how I could be so rude and thoughtless.

Dainah and I developed a really good relationship, and I often called her for any insight about her mother, her illnesses, her history, or how to deal with her. I was searching for help from anyone.

Dainah was very insightful and was always willing to

spend as much time with me on the phone as I needed. She was the one person who was able to keep me grounded through all the turbulence. There were occasions when I thought I was on the edge of coming apart at the seams. Without her support, I think I would have melted down.

I was still making calls to dentist offices on Deborah's behalf hoping to find a place that needed a dental hygienist. She discovered a position with the Veterans Affairs that sounded like a good job opportunity, and the drive would not be as brutal as the commute to Arvada. The job application process, however, was mind numbing and put a lot of pressure on Deborah. Finally, we got her application submitted but had no clue if it was correct, and then we never got a response. She said she expected as much. She was giving up hope of ever finding a permanent full-time job again.

We made a run to the annual Garden & Home Show in downtown Denver. Spring was fast approaching, and that meant planning to start work on the backyard of our new house. There had not been enough time the previous fall to do any yard work with our moving in late August, but we knew the homeowner association would want to see some activity before too long.

We found some good ideas and decided to tear out the deck stairs as they blocked our westward view from the walkout basement. Once torn down, I would build a new set of stairs on the northeast side of the house. We also agreed to have paver bricks installed versus running concrete for our patio. One of the best ideas from the home show was a flower planter made out of patio pavers. Deborah really liked that concept. We now had some ideas to work with but had no clue how expensive all of yard and patio work would be.

Deborah was really enjoying her monthly quilting classes and the women she was connecting with. She wanted to host the March gathering, so I made sure to schedule a trip to get some work done around the farm. I didn't want to be an annoyance to the quilting crew.

I was glad Deborah was involved with that group of gals. She looked forward to the get-togethers and needed those women to hang out with. One of her first projects was to make a quilt for her granddaughter, and she attacked the task with passion, spending many hours meticulously cutting squares.

We made the annual trip back to the farm for the Fourth of July weekend. Deborah did fairly well, but by the end of the visit I could tell she did not feel well. The farmhouse had an old air-conditioning system that was losing to the heat and humidity. She was becoming easily agitated from the conditions, and we decided it was best to get back to Denver sooner rather than later. On the trip, we experienced some good old-fashioned Midwestern thunderstorms. Deborah loved to watch the lightning in these kinds of storms.

When we got back there were more doctor's appointments and follow-up tests. Eventually, Deborah was referred to an ear, nose, and throat specialist. He was pretty confident he knew what was happening with Deborah, but more tests were needed, which meant a new round of steroids. Deborah was very upset with needing to go through another round of steroids, her seventh since February. But what was she to do?

The ENT doc told us Deborah's sinuses were packed with infection, which in turn was causing a lot of drainage. He thought this was compounding the asthma and led to the bronchitis that then led to pneumonia. The drainage and all the infection was going straight into her lungs. Yuck!

Deborah had previously endured sinus surgery, but our current specialist said he didn't think the surgery was successful. In other words, the previous surgery did not clean out all of her sinuses, which eventually led to more infections over the years and the severity of her current condition. Of course, this news really upset Deborah. She had butted heads with the doctor who performed her earlier surgery, and now she learned he hadn't even done a thorough job. We needed to schedule another sinus surgery.

July was especially difficult, and I was getting really frustrated. The tension in the house was escalating, and Deborah's anger could arise in a flash. The whole situation was becoming mind numbing and emotionally draining.

One time during a bout of anger she told me that I was the one who was bipolar. I thought about that and wondered if I was off my rocker, so I called Dainah again. I am not sure I would have been able to keep my faculties about me without Dainah's counsel. My mind and emotions felt like they could unravel at any time.

One Saturday evening, we went to services at a local church. We did this on occasion depending on our weekend plans. While walking through the parking lot and into the church out of the blue she said, "Isn't it terrible I hate people?"

I just thought to myself, "Yes, it is." Too often I could feel that hatred directed toward me.

Deborah knew she had a problem with anger and hatred and that it could blow in like a gale force wind. Someone could do something that was out of line in her mind at just the wrong time, and she would immediately build a wall of resentment and hatred toward that person. Usually they had no clue what they had done, and that someone was often me.

Deborah understood she was only hurting herself and she had to let her anger go and forgive people. Easier said than done! This was a difficult, difficult battle for her. Some people battle drugs. Some people battle alcohol. Deborah battled anger. The old saying is that being aware of your problem is half the battle. The other half is fixing the problem, and that is usually a herculean task.

There were days that I just sat at my desk in a daze. I literally went through the motions. I couldn't get any work done and could barely take calls. I don't think I made much sense to whomever I was talking to. I was worn out, confused, frustrated, and lost. There were many days like this, and they were happening more frequently. It was like being functionally comatose. All the conflicts with Deborah and then her constant illnesses were taking a toll on me. I could barely get work done to keep my business going. The struggle was becoming overwhelming.

It was also getting more difficult to come up with excuses when friends asked why I would not be able to make this event or that get-together. Often I would attend but without Deborah. There were only a couple of close friends to whom I hinted at what was happening in our lives. Other friends suspected something was not kosher.

Going for regular bike rides always helped me deal with stress. They were like therapy sessions; they gave me a break from the daily chaos and allowed me time to think, to pray, or to just clear my mind of clutter. Often on these rides, I dreamed of the single life, the way my life used to be.

I knew this wasn't easy for Deborah either. We were both hurting in our own separate ways but could not communicate our feelings to each other.

Even though Deborah and I had stopped going to counseling together, I still kept up my periodic visits with Rick for a check in. Sometimes I wanted to know what I could do to improve on my end to better our marriage. Other times I wanted feedback on what he thought was going on with Deborah and what I could do to help make life better for her. I just wanted to help.

I also visited friends with counseling backgrounds looking for advice or any bit of insight I could find. If I thought someone could help, I reached out to them for feedback. I even talked with pastor friends as I thought there might also be a spiritual element involved.

Everyone had good advice, but ultimately nothing really changed.

As I read through the book *Emotional Vampires*, I finally hit a section that offered answers. The book outlines a number of mental and emotional health disorders. Each chapter of the book has a self-analysis section to help you identify a problem and its severity.

Finally, I came to a section in which Deborah fit a majority of the checklist.

- A workaholic, check
- Has a hard time relaxing, check
- Can find something wrong with other's way of doing things, check
- Annoying attention to detail, check
- Gets upset when asked to deviate from routine, check
- Often feels overwhelmed by work, check

The list went on. Then the detailed description throughout the chapter explained what I experienced with Deborah. It appeared I was onto something. I thought I found the answer to Deborah's challenges. I hoped maybe now we could head down a path to help her, and I was kind of excited. Then I read a line in the book that said this condition does not respond to drugs. Maybe that is why, in time, the bipolar medications appeared to have no impact. Rick confirmed what I read.

When Deborah had confessed to Kenna her severe problems with depression and suicide, it was a gut punch for me. And now, I felt another blow to the solar plexus; I was crushed. How could there be no way to help Deborah? It did not seem fair or right or conceivable.

Helpless and Exhausted

Men are fixers. Too often men want to fix their wives' problems when their wives usually just want them to listen. I desperately wanted to help Deborah, but my hands were tied behind my back with a whole role of duct tape.

For several months, almost every night when I went to bed, I prayed for God to bring Deborah healing—any healing! I asked God to bring her healing from the physical pain and the mental pain. Any healing would be a dramatic improvement. Night after night I prayed, and yet Deborah was only getting sicker and more difficult to live with.

Then, by mid-July, I hit a breaking point; I was seriously ready to file for divorce. I truly didn't think I was going to survive mentally and emotionally. This time I was the one serious about divorce instead of Deborah. She had been the one to bring up divorce in the past anytime we got into a really bad place. I have no clue how close she ever really was to filing, but now I was ready to pull the ripcord and had some preliminary talks with a couple of attorneys.

I scheduled another counseling appointment, but this time I scheduled it with Kenna. I felt that I needed the female perspective one last time. My first question to her was, "Tell me why I should stay in this relationship?"

Her reply: "It sounds like you have made up your mind. What you are going to do?"

Ten minutes into an hour session, and we were essentially done. I would start the divorce process. Here I was, fifty years old, married for the first time and for only two years, and I was going to end it. I felt like a complete failure.

We continued talking, of course. I had paid my fee and was not leaving after only ten minutes. We talked about just how miserable Deborah's life appeared to be, the ongoing sicknesses, the multiple rounds of steroids, menopause, fights with me, anxiety with work, mental health issues. On and on and on!

At one point I said to Kenna in all seriousness, "Sometimes I wonder if Deborah would be better off dead."

Deborah was a Christian; her eternal destiny was secure, and she knew it. The ultimate hope of a Christian is eternal life in the company of our Savior Jesus Christ. It just seemed like life had become so extremely difficult for her on this earth that her physical death would be a relief from the unending pain and torment. In death, she would have the peace that surpasses all understanding.

The other issue I wanted some feedback on was an upcoming trip to Santa Barbara for my birthday. We were to spend a long weekend with our friends, Tim and Theresa. Deborah had instantly bonded with Theresa on our first vacation together, and she was looking forward to seeing both of them again.

We were going to stay along the California coast, visit some wineries, and see a play in Solvang. Tim and I had worked it out so we could also see Hearst Castle. As an aficionado of classic movies, Deborah was an especially big fan of the movie *Citizen Kane* and understood the role William Randolph Hearst played in the world of celebrities. This would be the highlight of the trip, and she was jazzed. She had always wanted to see the Hearst Castle.

Now, here I sat with Kenna, and I wasn't sure I even wanted Deborah to go along. She was in such bad moods and so angry with me most days that I could not see how we could have a good time together. On the other hand, I had to figure out how to explain all this to Tim and Theresa. What was I going to say to Deborah about the trip? How and when was I going to tell her about my decision to divorce?

I met with Kenna on Tuesday. On Thursday we were to fly out. There was little time to figure out how to deal with it all.

Driving home from work on Wednesday afternoon I had a

revelation, literally! Maybe you could call it a revealing. In all honesty, it would be more accurate to say that God punched me hard upside the head! A good old-fashioned haymaker. Whatever you want to call it, God got into my head in a big, clear, and unambiguous way. A thought exploded through my mind like a huge neon billboard:

"What Am I Doing?"

I married Deborah because I loved her. She was the only woman in my life I had dated who told me she loved me. I had taken a vow before God and Deborah. For better or for worse, I was committed to Deborah until death do us part.

And I had promised Deborah in counseling when she told us about the depression and suicide challenges that I would not leave her, no matter what! She had thought I would leave her if I found out about her struggles, but I made it clear that I was with her one hundred percent of the way. And after all of those promises was I now going to file for divorce? I felt like a hypocrite.

Driving home that day, I made a promise to God. I told Him that I knew Deborah was suffering, and even though life together could be difficult, even though I had no clue if it would get any better, *I'M All IN!!*

I was all in, and I made the decision not to divorce Deborah nor leave her, either now when she needs me the most or ever. For better or for worse, that was the vow. The pendulum had swung way over to the worse side, but I knew I had to honor the promise. I had made a covenant with God and Deborah. I would honor my promise in faith. There was no other option.

I would not, could not divorce Deborah. Discussion over!

I was excited, and I pounded the steering wheel at my newfound commitment.

That night at dinner Deborah was clearly upset. She was

very perceptive and knew I had been an unhappy camper. "Do you want me to go to California tomorrow?" she asked in a hurt tone.

That was not an easy question to answer, and before my epiphany I would have said no or come up with some buffoonish answer that sounded like no. But now I said, "Deborah, I would much rather have you go, than not go. But you have to decide. You have been super sick, and you have to decide if you can make the trip."

That's all it took. All Deborah needed to hear was that I was good with her going on our vacation. Her attitude changed, and without saying anything else that evening she went about packing her bags. The next morning, I was back in her good graces, and we were on our way to California.

We landed in Santa Barbara, and once Tim and Theresa found us at the airport, we headed out for lunch on one of the piers. We then hung around the town for a while. Deborah and Theresa went shopping, and Tim and I went looking for a local microbrewery.

While walking a few blocks to our car, I noticed that Tim and I got way ahead of Deborah and Theresa. We stopped and waited for them to catch up, and then we all walked together. The pace was extremely slow, and I realized Deborah was having a difficult time breathing. Sinus surgery could not come soon enough.

That evening we drove up to Pismo Beach and stayed in a room overlooking the Pacific Ocean. The next day we headed to Hearst Castle for the big tour. The place is so big they break the tours up into three or four options. Deborah and I took the beginner tour while Tim and Theresa took another tour since they had been there a couple of times already. Deborah was so excited about Hearst Castle that she could hardly contain herself. It was definitely an amazing place, and the story behind it was equally amazing.

After the tour we headed to the wine country where we

had rented a seaside cottage. We found a local market and bought a bunch of cheese, crackers, and other food items and proceeded to have a fun afternoon on the cottage patio enjoying our time together and the beautiful, cool coastal weather.

We spent Saturday night in Solvang where the local theater company put on a performance of *West Side Story*. It was a good production. By evening the weather had turned really cold, which affected Deborah's breathing. We bundled her up with some extra jackets and scarfs.

We flew back that Sunday.

Staying with Deborah in the cottage on our trip, I had my first direct experience with what she dealt with each night back home. She had been sleeping in the guest bedroom, so I didn't know how bad things had gotten. It wasn't long after getting in bed that Deborah had difficulty breathing and needed her inhaler. Then she realized she was not going to be able to sleep. She had brought along her laptop and a number of movies just for this potential situation. Lying flat made it hard for her to breathe, so the solution was to get up, or sit up, and watch a movie.

Since there was a desk and a big chair in the room, we gathered all the extra pillows and blankets and Deborah sat at the desk. Propped up in the chair with the pillows and blankets, she could watch movies in a soft cushy set-up and be comfortable. Then she could fall asleep while upright and be able to breath better.

Needless to say, Deborah was awake watching movies for a long time, which meant I could not get to sleep. The next morning my hind end was dragging from lack of sleep. It was then that I started to comprehend just how difficult Deborah's life had become. Her nights at home in the front bedroom consisted of this routine nearly every evening.

Fatigue always makes me a cranky and unpleasant person. Now I began to understand where some of Deborah's crankiness and anger was coming from. She was constantly exhausted. She lived with fatigue every day. How long had it been since she had had a full night's sleep? Three months or six months, or was it longer? I can't say exactly, but it was a long time.

In getting to know Deborah I came to understand that she was a tough cookie. Rarely did she miss work, and few obstacles stopped her from doing what she thought needed to be done. But this was beyond what most people could handle on a daily basis. I honestly don't know how she did it, and I kept earnestly praying for God to bring her some relief and healing.

Something had changed between Deborah and I in just the few days during the trip. The fighting stopped; we were communicating better and with less tension.

Deborah was also excited about the upcoming surgery and the idea that just maybe she would be able to get back to normal after the procedure.

After we returned from our California trip Deborah sent Dainah an e-mail:

Hi sweetie!!

How are my girls doing? How many accidents has Bela had this week? I saw an Elmo DVD: *Elmo in Grouchland*. I'll buy it for her.

We had soooo much fun in California! We met our friends Tim and Theresa in Santa Barbara. They live in Bakersfield, and they drove up to pick us up at the airport and we then from there we went north to San Simeon and did Hearst Castle which was INCREDIBLE. If you guys ever go to Cali, you have to do it. And we went to the many vineyards and did taste testing. On another day we went to a town called Solvang, which is an old Dutch town with several old Dutch shops. That night we saw *West Side Story* by local summerstock actors and many times walked by the ocean. One night we stayed in a high-rise resort, and our room looked out on the beach. On the second night we stayed in a seaside resort spa, and it was REALLY nice, but the last night sucked.

Well, on to the next business. I met with ENT and we reviewed my CAT scan on Monday. I still have pus in the bottom third of most of my sinuses, and I have a bad fungal infection in all of them. Apparently, only one of eight sinuses opened and was cleaned up from the last surgery. So, he is going to be fairly aggressive this time and open them all so I can drain and maybe fix my septum if it looks like it's contributing. My surgery is on Monday in the morning, and I'll be home in the afternoon. I'm back on steroids for the seventh time in six months and antibiotics for the fifth time. I told them this is it!! I have put on 25 pounds (all belly fat) directly related to cortisol. I have lost handfuls of hair, it makes me extremely moody, and my blood pressure goes sky high!! You are never supposed to be on steroids more than twice in a single year. I was pissed!!!

This has been the worst year for me. I'm gonna call it my LOST YEAR.

Well, honey, I'm done complaining. Have a great week and kiss my sweet pea for me. Tell her that Grandma D loves her!

MOM

9

DEPARTURE

"This is the end. I am going. I am leaving now. Goodbye!"

—Bilbo Baggins, *The Lord of the Rings*

Deborah thought there was a real possibility of her dying while in surgery. I thought she was being a little nutty and dramatic, but we talked about the possibility. She expressed that she wanted to be cremated. Unknown to me at the time she wrote out some instructions for her mom and kids:

Okay, I'm having sinus surgery on Monday. Lungs still inflamed, coughing, wheezing, intubation may not go well. If I die, I told Josh to cremate me (cost being an issue). *No* arguments, people! Mom, come and help Josh go through my things. Mom, Michael, Dainah, come and get the things you want of mine. Josh is okay with that. (Mike, you can leave it here until you have a place to store it.)

This is not in any way Josh's or anybody else's fault! I'm human and crap happens. We all die someday. I'm definitely in a much better place and feeling great now! I'm with the Lord waiting for all of my family who are Christians to come on their appointed day. If such things are allowed, I'll be there to greet you. Those of you who aren't Christian, think about it—Heaven or Hell. To me, it's a no-brainer. Love you, Mom

In the same journal she listed three people she planned to write letters of forgiveness to before her surgery. She also wrote about her struggles with certain people and listed other people she was praying for. She closed with:

I slept two hours last night and coughed and wheezed the rest of the time! Lord, please give me respite and seven hours sleep without coughing and wheezing tonight! I would really appreciate it!

I pray that You will allow me to have my surgery on Monday so I can recover from my illnesses—please! Amen.

This leads us to the night she again came into our bedroom and woke me, exclaiming, "Josh, I think I'm having a heart attack."

Deborah had some heart issues to go along with all her other health challenges and woke up in the middle of the night convinced she had had a heart attack. My first reaction was to load up and head to the emergency room, but she wouldn't go. She was afraid her sinus surgery would be cancelled if we went to the emergency room complaining of having a heart attack, and she was desperate for sinus surgery and hopefully some relief.

Finally, she asked, "Can I get in bed with you?" Well, I would have rather had her in bed with me every night over the past several months, but for my benefit, that didn't happen.

On the day of surgery, her recovery room stay lasted much longer than expected. When the surgeon came out around 10:30 a.m. to visit with me, he explained that she had had two major asthma attacks coming out of anesthesia. They decided to keep her longer for observation.

Later that day, Deborah told me that when she woke up from surgery she immediately could not breathe and was grabbing at people to warn them. She was panicking but without any good way of telling someone what was happening. They got her under control, and then it happened again a short time later. At one point, she said she actually thought she was going to die.

Recovery from that point went well, and Deborah was feeling much better. Mike was coming to visit for a couple of weeks later that month, and during that time we were going to drive out to Utah to spend a long weekend with her mom.

Also, that month was our one year anniversary of moving into Deborah's dream home. We both loved our new house. Quite frankly, I never thought I would ever live in a home like it. Growing up out on the Stinking Water Creek in southwest Nebraska, the family home was quite small in hindsight, but for me it was normal. Our home made both of us happy, but especially Deborah. On the night of our move-in anniversary, we went out for a relaxing dinner to celebrate.

Before we left for Utah, we had a follow-up consultation with the surgeon. Once he finished the post-surgical exam, he declared the surgery a complete success. He said her sinuses were clear and looked great. He was confident that most of the other health issues Deborah had been dealing with were related to her infected sinuses and the ugly drainage going into her lungs. He said she should feel better and better as time went by.

Well, Deborah was feeling better for sure, and she appeared livelier and more energetic than I had seen her in a long time. The news from the surgeon left us both excited and relieved. Maybe we had an answer for her terrible health struggles that she had been through during the past year and the path to healing was before us.

On the Road Again

Deborah, Mike, Otto, and I loaded up and headed for Utah to visit Deborah's mom, Ina. We were in no hurry, so we made a loop up over Loveland Pass. Otto loved hanging out the window while sitting on Deborah's lap. The fresh air was enticing for him, and he tried to lean out the window as far as he could. Mike was concerned that he was going to fall out and get run over, but Deborah held onto his hind legs tightly.

After a stop for lunch and a quick stretch, we were back in the car. Deborah started getting playful, poking me in the ribs and trying to tickle me. One time I blocked her arm too hard, which knocked it against her mouth and cut the inside of her lip. Now her lip was bleeding, her eyes were tearing up, and I felt like an ass. I had no clue what Mike was thinking sitting in the back seat, but I was sure he was not impressed with me. The rest of the drive was quiet. We made it to Ina's house in time for dinner and settled in for the evening.

Saturday was our second anniversary. I had a difficult time finding the right card for Deborah. I was up well before Deborah and took Otto for our early morning walk. When I came back she was still asleep, so I whispered, "Happy Anniversary, Punk'n" and slipped her the card. She mumbled, "I love you."

The inside of my card to Deborah read:

The Lord has been so good to us.
He's blessed us far beyond our walk with Him.
He's worthy of all our praise
on our anniversary.

The Lord poured out His blessing
upon me when He brought you into my life.
You're a treasure whom I cherish and adore.
You've made life much more enjoyable.

I feel totally complete with you.
I thank the Lord for giving me a godly,
virtuous woman and a beautiful one at that!

I knew the card would mean a lot to Deborah after the way the year had gone.

Otto and I headed out for another morning walk to the park. While we were at the park, Deborah had gotten out of bed and dressed and stepped out onto the stoop. She saw us up on the hill and flashed us her beautiful smile and waved.

That evening we went out for our second anniversary dinner, and we insisted that Ina go with us. There was a new restaurant in Price. It was a nice dinner, and we enjoyed our time together. Back at the house, Deborah watched an old movie while I got ready for bed.

I found an anniversary card on the nightstand. It was a classic and made me laugh as it was dead-on:

Happy Anniversary
to my HUSBAND
I've stolen covers till you froze
Changed my hair, my shoes, my clothes . . .
I've lost it when I'm PMS-ing—Just leave me ALONE!
May have nagged when I'm obsessing—Do I have to do everything
around here?!
I've run up hefty shopping bills
And criticized your driving skills . . .
So, I think it's time to say to you . . .
Hey, I'm your wife—that's what I do!
Happy Anniversary
I Love You

I gave Deborah a big thank you smooch for the great card. I told her I loved her and was sorry for hurting her lip. She reminded me once again that she was not one of my old college buddies and that I needed to try to take it a little easier when playing around. I agreed and then headed to bed while she stayed up watching her movie in the living room.

Deborah came into the bedroom at least once, if not twice, to use her inhaler. Not long after her sinus surgery I noticed Deborah using her inhaler more. In the back of my mind I wondered about this and was a bit concerned. Deborah never mentioned it, so I didn't ask any questions. Ignorance is bliss, right?

Eventually Deborah came to bed. Sometime around 4:30 a.m. she got up and took Otto out to pee. I have no clue why she got up with Otto then, as she had never taken him out that early before. Maybe Otto woke her up. When they came back in the house, Otto refused to come back into the bedroom, so Deborah in a gruff, whispering command told me to get up and help her. Otto was in the hall and for some weird reason resisted coming back into the bedroom. With some effort, I was able to get him to return and go back to bed.

We lay back down, but now I couldn't sleep, and we were in her twin bed. There was not a lot of room to move around. Since I didn't want to turn over and roll on Deborah's hair I kind of petted her head to see where her hair was in the dark. In kind of a stern voice, Deborah asked, "What are you doing?" and I told her I did not want to roll over on her hair.

It was now after five, and I still couldn't get back to sleep, so I gingerly got out of bed, left the room, and went and lay down on the couch in the living room. I was afraid my tossing and turning would wake Deborah or keep her awake. Sleeping did not go well on the couch. I was extremely restless for some reason and lay there wide awake.

Around seven, I'd had it. I got up and quietly went down the hall, slowly opened the bedroom door and whispered for Otto to come out. I got Otto's leash, and took him for our morning walk. When we got back to the house, Ina and Mike were up. I fed Otto and made myself breakfast. While sitting at the kitchen table I happened to glance up at the clock. It was nine, and Deborah was not up. Not a peep or sound. That was not normal.

Internally, alarm bells started to howl and panic set in. Without saying anything, I immediately got up and headed down the hall with anxiety washing over me like a tidal wave. Slowly I opened the door. The room was still pretty dark as the shades were pulled. I could see Deborah still lying in bed. She was in the exact same position as she was earlier.

I slowly approached her and whispered, "Punk'n. Punk'n." It was dark, but I could see something wasn't right. Deborah had poor circulation and was always somewhat cold, but now she was really cold to the touch. I felt for a pulse on her wrist. Nothing.

In a full panic, I hollered for someone to dial 911 while running down the hall. I was the first to the phone. Immediately Ina and Mike headed for Deborah's bedroom. I had a hard time with the 911 call center, probably from my state of panic, and I could not remember Ina's address. They kept asking questions, and I couldn't give coherent answers. "Just get here now!"

Ina and Mike were giving Deborah CPR. Mike came out and took over the 911 call, and I helped Ina give Deborah CPR, pleading for her to respond. "Come on, Punk'n! Come on!"

I wanted to believe she would respond, but intuitively I knew she would not. Later, we were told she had suffered death by natural causes with secondary chronic asthma. It is also possible that she experienced an embolism in her lungs.

The EMTs showed up after what seemed like an eternity. They took over, and we left the bedroom. The situation was surreal. I told myself this wasn't happening, but in the back of my mind I knew the reality we were facing. At some point the EMTs came out and told us what no husband, mother, or son ever wants to hear: Deborah was gone. She had most likely died three hours earlier, not long after I left the bedroom to sleep on the couch.

Shock, anguish, and disbelief blanketed me: a whirling, swirling mix of excruciating pain.

As the ambulance pulled out of the driveway, I stood on the stoop and whispered goodbye to my beautiful wife.

That was a black day. It was the hardest day of my life and the beginning of an extremely difficult journey.

Grief

Emotional and mental devastation must be similar to a hurricane making landfall or a tornado wiping clean an entire town. Both leave a concentrated path of catastrophic destruction.

Eventually I ended up on the back stoop and broke down completely. All the negative thoughts I had—divorce, dreaming about the single life, my words to Kenna at our last session before the California trip, and more—came flooding into my mind and dragged me into a deep, dark pit. My words in my last session with Kenna continuously flashed through my mind: "Sometimes I wonder if Deborah would not be better off dead."

I felt like my innards were being yanked out by meathooks. Regret is ugly, and death is irreversible. It was mentally and emotionally crushing.

Two years of marriage to the day, and Deborah was gone. How could this be?

The police were still at the house getting statements from each of us, but it took a long time before I could gather myself to talk.

I tried multiple times to call my mom, but she did not answer. I knew she was probably still at church. Finally, she answered, and I had to give her the shocking news. Then I called Tim and Theresa; then I called Deborah's best girlfriends

Becky and Monica. Everyone was in a state of disbelief. This was difficult news to tell people.

My mom and three sisters had fallen in love with Deborah in a short time and thought the world of her. Even with her mental health issues, they thought of her as a daughter and a sister. They adored her spunky personality and loved her big beautiful smile. Her death was devastating for them as well.

I was in no state to make a bunch of calls, so I started texting friends and family members. I asked my mom to have my sisters call different friends back home in Nebraska. Some close friends called throughout the day, but the calls were very difficult and emotionally draining. It was beyond overwhelming. I could not wrap my head around the thought of never seeing my beautiful wife again.

Mike or Ina had connected with Dainah in Indianapolis, and we had a short visit on the phone. She made travel plans to get to Utah as soon as possible, but she would not get to Ina's house until around midnight.

The day slogged along, and my pain whipped around like a cyclone. Part of the time, Ina, Mike, and I just sat in the living room somewhat comatose. I took several walks with Otto to break up the waiting. It was a long, silent, and difficult evening for all of us as we waited for Dainah to arrive.

Nothing seemed real; it all felt like a bad dream. It was like the earth had been knocked off its axis.

Ina had lived in Price most of her adult life and had a lot of friends in town. People were wonderful. They came by to offer their condolences, drop off food, and try to help in any way they could. They were just like the folks back in my hometown.

Eventually Dainah and Bela made it to Price. They arrived around midnight. We had time to talk a bit and everyone got their hugs in, and then it was time for bed. It was past midnight, but I couldn't have gone to sleep any earlier. I needed complete and total exhaustion to even attempt to go to sleep.

The sun rose Monday morning. I wanted to believe everything had been a dream and that Deborah would come out of the bedroom at any time. But that wasn't reality.

My dream girl, the girl I waited forty-eight years for, had left my life never to return. The girl I promised God I would never leave had departed.

There was comfort amidst the agony, and that was Deborah's faith.

They say time heals all wounds, but death is like the amputation of a limb. The wound may heal, but there is always a sense that the limb is still there.

> *I walked a mile with Pleasure;*
> *She chattered all the way,*
> *But left me none the wiser*
> *For all she had to say.*
> *I walked a mile with Sorrow,*
> *And not a word said she;*
> *But oh, the things I learned from her*
> *When Sorrow walked with me!*
>
> —Robert Browning Hamilton

10

SAYING GOODBYE

"It's not about you."

—Rick Warren, *The Purpose Driven Life*

One of the tasks we had planned to accomplish while in Price was to bring back a number of Deborah's belongings that were stored at her mom's house. Deborah also planned to bring along some of her dad's stuff that Ina didn't want. In advance, I had arranged to rent a small U-Haul trailer to pull back to Colorado with all of the stuff.

I picked up and paid for the trailer and somehow managed to back it down Ina's driveway to the garage without destroying anything. Credit my dad for teaching me how to drive trucks and tractors and to pull equipment on the farm.

Saturday, Mike and I had loaded up Deborah's stuff as well as her dad's band saw and welder. The U-Haul was packed.

Now, after the devastating events that night, I realized I was not going to be in any kind of condition, physically or mentally, to drive all the way back to Denver pulling the trailer. So, I called U-Haul and explained what had happened; I asked if I could return the trailer. They were, of course, very kind and understanding and agreed to let me return the rig, so we proceeded to unload everything.

While sitting with the lady at the U-Haul office going through the return paperwork, I noticed a cross on the wall. I asked her if she was a Christian, and she said yes. Knowing Deborah would insist on a Christian funeral and burial I asked her if she could recommend a Christian church or pastor. She recommended Pastor Dan at Price Chapel.

Finding the number for Price Chapel was easy; tracking down Pastor Dan was not so easy. It was Sunday afternoon and long after church services were over. Monday was his day off. I left a message at the church, and a few hours later one of the office assistants called me back to arrange a meeting with Pastor Dan for Monday evening. He was very gracious with his time.

Ina had also set an appointment for us with the funeral home. This appointment included going to the cemetery and selecting a burial plot. There were no available plots near Deborah's dad, but we did find a nice alternative. Price cemetery is a peaceful place.

We then went shopping for a dress for Deborah, which, of course, had to be green.

I did what had to be done, but it all seemed surreal. This was not how Deborah and I had planned to wrap up our second anniversary weekend. Deborah, Mike, Otto, and I were supposed to be on the road driving to Denver this very day, and here I was preparing for her funeral. It wasn't right!

We discussed arrangements including songs for the funeral service. Deborah had downloaded a Christian song for her ring tone on her new iPhone. It was a great tune and included the lyrics "I know my Redeemer lives." I knew that we had to have that song for her service, but I had no idea who wrote or performed it.

We planned Deborah's service in Price for Saturday, September 4. We needed to give family and friends a bit more time to make the trip to Price. I had a number of friends coming from Nebraska, California, and Colorado and some of Deborah's family was also coming from outside of Utah.

I went about writing Deborah's obituary with input from Ina, Dainah, and Mike. That is just one of the sad aspects about Deborah's illnesses; they overshadowed the beautiful soul that was inside her. The stress of life would sweep over her like a prairie fire and leave a charred landscape; sometimes the beauty was unrecognizable. She had many wonderful qualities that were overwhelmed by her illnesses. Her funeral, though, allowed us the opportunity to share them. The obituary was the time to honor her.

With five days until the service I knew I needed to head back to Colorado to catch up on some of my work and take care of personal business relating to Deborah's death. I also needed to start making arrangements for a memorial service in Denver. Plus, I needed to keep trying to reach more friends of Deborah's to let them know what happened.

It was a long, lonely drive back. Deborah had made the trip between Denver and Price many times, and one of her favorite stops along the way was a rest area called Bair Ranch in Glenwood Canyon. It's a nice quiet place along the Colorado River. Otto and I made a long stop there. It was a beautiful day and calm. We found a secluded area and hung out in the sun for a while—thinking, praying, crying.

Greif is a kaleidoscope of emotions: despair, helplessness, anger, frustration, anxiety, depression, confusion, loneliness, anguish, sadness, and guilt. Then, throw in the physical and mental fatigue.

Deborah regularly listened to Christian music radio stations, but I almost never did. Now, on this drive, contemporary Christian music was the only music I could listen to. It carried me back to Denver.

Ina and Dainah were busy in Price putting together the final details of the funeral service, and I was able to arrange a memorial service for Friday, September 10, at Cherry Hills Community Church. They had picked two more perfect songs for the services: "Amazing Grace" by Michael W. Smith and "How Great Thou Art" by Alan Jackson. Dainah thought she had discovered who sang "I Know My Redeemer Lives." It was Nicole C. Mullins.

The days were busy. I had to go through all of Deborah's stuff, gather and e-mail pictures to the funeral home for the service brochure, call our attorney, and do multiple rewrites of Deborah's obituary. I wanted to make sure that the song was the same as on Deborah's phone, so I drove down to the local Christian bookstore. They loaded up the song for me to listen to with a pair of headphones. Once the song started, I completely melted down sobbing. That was the song on Deborah's cell phone; the emotions hit me like a dump truck. The evenings were terribly difficult; it's hard to sleep when you are weeping profusely, and a soggy pillow does not make for a good place to rest a weary head.

On Wednesday (four days after Deborah died), my mom and sisters drove to Denver from Nebraska.

Revealing Insight

It's interesting what you learn about someone once they have died. The stories people tell about the person who passed on sometimes offer new insights and perspectives. People you didn't know but who knew your friend or family member well can provide many insights.

When my dad died, I learned new things about him from the many cards people wrote to my mom. I learned how much my dad meant to so many people in different ways. It was humbling and eye-opening. My dad and I had grown apart a bit over the years, and all those letters rekindled my love and respect for him. I appreciated even more who he was and tried to emulate his ways.

Dainah and Ina wanted me to gather some old family items while I was back in Denver: pictures, jewelry, mementos. In the process, I found two journals Deborah had written that were stored away in boxes.

I knew Deborah wrote prayer journals and prayer letters. This was one of the ways she communicated with God and let Him know her joys, heartaches, frustrations, and challenges. When we were married, occasionally I would come across a journal lying around. Wondering what it was I'd take a look and quickly close it knowing it was her personal time with God. Then I would never see it again. The same thing would happen with her prayer letters.

Once she was gone and I found the prayer journals and realized what they were, I read them all. It took time, but it was revealing. I learned many things about her that I never knew before. I wondered if only I had understood more about her difficulties, fears, and struggles maybe I could have been a better husband and been more helpful.

Sept. 27, 2007: I have a *big* headache tonight. I'm so tired of being sick. I'm asking Sean for a script for Cepthlexin tomorrow.

Oct. 16, 2007: I'm sick! Son-of-a-sea cook! So, I'm taking Clindamycin for 10 days and tomorrow I have to get my flu shot. Yuck! I'm so tired and worn out.

Oct. 25, 2007: I can't take it anymore! My sinuses are killing me, so I started taking prednisone.

Dec. 5, 2007: Life sucks, and I'm so tired of trying. If I had the drugs to end it, I would. I have been in pain for two weeks straight now, and today it's been the worst. The pain wears me down. I can't seem to do the right thing with Josh. I should cut it off. He deserves someone so much better than me.

Dec. 12, 2007: My chest (heart) hurts again and I'm having arrhythmias again—I know I should have an echo done, but on the other hand if my mitral valve gives out then I don't have to worry about tomorrow, do I? God let me come home!

May 8, 2008: I'm so stressed out today. My neck & back are killing me—even my lower back, which I never have trouble with, is killing me. The girls at work said I looked like I was going to cry!

May 14, 2008: I have been living on the edge today! Exhausted and in severe pain with my entire back, neck, head, and TMJ. I thought I'd never make it through the day. Everybody was especially trying. I seriously need some Valium to relax my body. I'm so exhausted.

There are many more entries dealing with Deborah's physical pain. Physically she was wracked from her professional career, and then there were heart issues and other ailments I was not aware of. I didn't really understand the side effects of different medicines until I read about them in her journals.

I knew Deborah would usually take about six ibuprofens just to get the physical pain under control so she could sleep, and getting enough sleep was always a challenge for her. Eventually our doctor prescribed Gabapentin to help with the pain, which certainly helped, but there were side effects that caused other complex problems. There never seemed to be a complete fix for any of her health issues. One potential solution would cause other problems, and around and around we went.

Then there was the emotional and mental pain.

Oct. 3, 2007: I killed a bunny with my car tonight, and I cried buckets! Why me—why can't someone else be a bunny killer? I'm stressed this week, and I don't know why!! Please God help me to calm down give me Your strength, comfort, peace!

Nov. 2, 2007: I'm emotionally out of sorts today. Not wanting to talk to or see Josh. Why?

April 20, 2008: Grant died. Josh is sulking and is now *NOT* going to Indy. He's doing it to hurt me not because he feels obligated to go to the funeral. My joy is seriously hurt.

May 5, 2008: I wish I could disappear on an island or remote village somewhere. A place where no one knows me. The last time I felt like running away was somewhere between 1984 and 1986. Can't quite pin down the year, just the era. Secretly wishing to disappear and be a nobody. Would anyone miss me???

May 7, 2008: GOD, I WISH I WERE DEAD. I can't take all this pressure—WORK—HEALTH—RELATIONSHIP. It's just too much.

May 10, 2008: It's so hard to tell Josh how fragile I am. That I'm always on the edge of getting my heart totally broken beyond repair.

The poor girl couldn't find relief, and I was only minutely aware of just how much pain she was really in. Deborah didn't talk much about her problems, perhaps out of pride or fear of what people might think. Most likely she didn't want me and her family to worry about her. She didn't tell anyone about her lifelong struggle with severe depression and battle with temptations of suicide until she was forty-nine years old.

One of the things that made Deborah so beautiful was her emotional sensitivity. That same sensitivity could work against her, or me, or others.

I warned Deborah early in our relationship that I had a unique ability to say hurtful things to people without even being aware of it. Sometimes I would try to be funny, sometimes flippant, but all too often the result was not as I intended. She chuckled and didn't take me too seriously, but I could really throw her on an emotional roller coaster. As usual I was often oblivious to what was happening inside of her.

I remember the bunny killing incident. Deborah called me crying and told me what happened. I laughed about it! In my worldview there were an estimated 30 billion bunnies in the Denver area alone. Who cares if someone ran over one? There were multitudes more in the bunny pipeline waiting to take its place. Well, my chuckling only knocked Deborah into a deeper state of despair, plus it made her mad at me for being so uncaring. Geez! This was all new territory for me.

But there was one entry that set me back on my heels:

May 16, 2008: I am feeling like "it" is close. I can feel it, and I'm scared and happy. Almost everyone I care about is saved now, and I know I won't perish! But I am disappointed that I won't see my grandkids grow up. I won't see Mike married, and I won't get to spend the rest of my life with Josh.

I read it several times. It was hard to believe.

Deborah knew her time on earth was near the end, and she knew it several months before we planned to get married. I was stunned! She never confided in me anything of this sort. I thought we were going to get old together. Once in a while when walking into church I would crack a joke about some old couple hobbling into the building. I'd say, "That's us in thirty years." Deborah knew better; that was never going to happen.

It made me wonder why she was so excited to get married when she knew her time was about up. The only thing I could think of is that just like my going to the singles event the night we met, someone was pushing her along.

In hindsight, I can say there were hints along the way that she knew she might die soon. The most recent was her adamant belief that she would not survive the sinus surgery.

During the summer, in the months before her death, Deborah spent a lot of time reading obituaries online, mainly of the *Salt Lake Tribune* and her hometown paper. She mostly read about people around our age and often made comments about the deaths. I remember thinking her new interest seemed a bit odd; but mostly, it was in one ear and out the other.

There was also one conversation we had just a couple of weeks before she died. We sat down to eat and began talking about different life issues. Out of the blue she asked me if we got divorced would I ever date again. It was a peculiar question because we were now in the best place we had ever been during our marriage. But once again, I let the questions slip by and didn't think much about it.

I was just too blind and uninformed to understand Deborah's physical, mental, and spiritual state. She wanted to go home to heaven. How I saw life was not how Deborah saw life. And only after she was gone could I understand.

For me life was pretty good. Business was going well, I had married my dream girl, and lived in a beautiful home. Why would you not want to live and enjoy life?

Dog Bonding

An interesting thing happened—or did not happen—with Otto.

Otto and Deborah were like two peas in a pod. Wherever Deborah went there was Otto. Whatever car they were in, he was on her lap. In the house when Deborah was in her recliner, he was on her lap or sitting next to her. They were almost inseparable. Like Deborah, Otto is also emotionally sensitive. And they had the same color of eyes. It was like they were soul mates.

You've heard stories about pets mourning after their owner dies. The emotional bond between a pet owner and a pet, especially a dog, goes deep. And when the bond is broken by the death of the pet owner, the dog can go through a mourning process as well, just like humans.

Interestingly, Otto never showed a sign of missing Deborah. He was as normal as could be. It was odd, and I noticed it right away. In fact, when I would come home after being gone for a while, Otto would go completely bonkers with excitement upon seeing me. He had never shown any such excitement with me in the seven months we had him before Deborah died. I almost had the feeling that she told him goodbye, not to miss her, and to take care of me.

As time moved on, Otto's presence was a blessing. Many days, I would come home from the office tired, depressed, and in a dark fog. I would hear his excited yelps as I pulled into the garage. And when I walked in the door, his excitement was the only possible thing in the world that could cause a smile to appear on my face and produce some level of joy. I believe Deborah finding Otto was part of God's plan. Without my understanding, Otto was taking care of me in my time of mourning.

Revelation: The Ultimate Plan

We wrapped up the final details of the Utah funeral. Ina and Dainah did a great job of organizing things. Our mothers had never met, and now was the first opportunity for them to do so. Family and friends arrived from around the country.

The Price service was set for Saturday morning, September 4. The service outline included the songs Ina and Dainah selected. Mike read Deborah's obituary, and he talked about his relationship with his mom. Then I was to speak and tell our story. Pastor Dan would give the sermon.

While sitting in the front pew of the chapel waiting for the service to start, with Deborah's open casket just a few feet in front of me, I had a moment of clarity. This whole thing was God's plan. Reading Deborah's prayer journals provided the answers and brought all the other pieces of the puzzle together.

Deborah knew her time to head to her heavenly home was near—even before we were engaged. She knew! All the things she was suffering from were causing her incomprehensible pain, and it was only getting worse with time. When I read her journal entries, I got the sense of someone completely over-whelmed and weighed down with this temporal life.

All of her sufferings were also making it next to impossible for her to work. After she was fired from her full-time job, she struggled to find another permanent job. Even at her favorite job she wrote about being overcome with anxiety, and she only worked there one day a week. Physically, emotionally, and mentally, the toll of work, even part-time, was becoming too much for her handle.

In an instant, sitting in the pew, it was completely clear to me why God brought us together, and it wasn't about me.

From the day we met until the day she departed there was a master plan in place.

Certainly, God answered my prayer: He brought Deborah

into my life, ultimately blessing me with marriage. I prayed unceasingly for years, twenty years to the day almost. Certainly, I benefited tremendously from my marriage to Deborah. I learned more over the three years and four months we were together—from the night we met until the day she died—than I learned the forty-six years before we met.

Deborah changed my life kind of like a tsunami changes a beach; it washes away a lot of junk but also some good things. Ultimately, new possibilities are exposed.

But the reality is that I believe God brought us together primarily for her benefit and protection. He knew perfectly her pain and struggles and that life was only getting more difficult for her each day. I believe He brought us together so she could live in a secure place and be loved until He called her home.

For one year, she was able to live in her dream home, and she didn't have to work to survive.

If we had not met, I don't know how Deborah would have made things work financially with her job situation and her health challenges. Because of God's plan, she was in a situation where she did not have to work full-time, and she lived in her new house where she could find some relief and a bit of happiness until God came for her.

But Deborah was truly the one God was watching over. He answered her prayers completely.

In Deborah's prayer journals, there were multiple entries asking God to bring her home. The pains of life were becoming just too much of a burden. She had an idea that the time was close, but she did not know the day that He would snatch her away.

When things were going as bad as ever between us, from late winter and into summer, I prayed as earnestly as I had ever in my life for God to bring Deborah healing—physical healing, mental healing, emotional healing, and spiritual healing. Any healing! I begged God to bring to her relief in some way shape or form. That is what I asked for—Deborah's healing—but I was thinking in the here and now.

I also prayed that I would be a good husband and not cause her more stress. I prayed that I would know how to help her.

God answered all of those prayers of mine, just not how I was expecting or wanting. Our answered prayers were not about me, but about Him and about her. And He answered them in His time. He brought Deborah full and complete healing, and He did so by bringing her home to Him.

God answered Deborah's prayers exactly as she asked.

Deborah was a relatively new Christian, at least in my book. She accepted Jesus Christ as her Savior only a couple of years before we met. She believed in Jesus, who He said He was and why He came to this earth and what His long-term plan was.

She was extremely serious about her faith and completely committed to God—as much as anyone I have known. In her short Christian life she probably studied the Bible more than most Christians do in their lifetime. Her devotion to knowing God and leaning on Jesus is an example for all Christians to emulate. Her Bible is highlighted throughout and marked up with notes; she wanted to know and understand God as well as she possibly could.

Today, she rejoices in the presence of her Savior, Jesus Christ, and is totally healed as she and I prayed for in our separate ways.

Ultimately, both our prayers were answered.

> *The Savior can solve every problem,*
> *The tangles of life can undo.*
> *There's nothing too hard for Jesus;*
> *There's nothing that He cannot do.*

—Author Unknown

11

CLOSURE

"The essence of life is change, a panoply of growth and decay. Elect life and growth, and you elect change and the prospect of death."

—M. Scott Peck, *The Road Less Traveled*

In our daily lives, whether personally or professionally, closure means bringing something to a conclusion or an end. Webster's Dictionary calls closure "an act of closing: the condition of being closed" or "a bringing to a stopping point, finished, to bring to an end."

Take, for example, the world of financial planning or specifically helping someone implement an estate plan. The client needs a basic will, a general durable power of attorney, health care power of attorney as well as a living will, and possibly different types of trusts from a revocable living trust to an irrevocable life insurance trust. All of these are the basics of an estate plan.

With the assistance of a skilled estate planning attorney, a financial planner can help a client develop a comprehensive plan to determine how and when and to whom his belongings are distributed. A person can set out instructions of how his estate is to be managed in case of disability or some other incapacity, and he can also direct end of life planning circumstances in advance. Implementing an estate plan also relieves his survivors from a lot of stress and conflict.

To execute the estate plan, all the documents must be signed and notarized and assets re-titled and transferred to trusts in order to have its desired effect. When all the steps and procedures are finished; the estate plan is finished. We could say there is closure.

If you have ever bought a house, you understand the time and work involved. Once you have the keys to your new home, you can say there is closure. A similar but even more complex process occurs in the world of commerce when one business buys another business.

Long ago, two people might come to an agreement with a handshake. You would know that a man's handshake was as good as his word, and there would be closure. You could trust that the agreement was complete. Nowadays, during these complex transactions, kinks often arise that cause problems. Even when some unforeseen circumstances come up, that doesn't mean that one party can get out of the contract to which they are legally bound. Often people, for whatever reason, try to skirt their part of an agreement. In such cases, even when there are legal documents involved, closure is not always so simple or quickly achieved. So it is with grief.

Too often, I think people on the outside expect those grieving the loss of a loved one to find closure in a short time —maybe a year or even less. I used to assume so.

When my dad died in 2003, I knew my mom was lonely and in pain. But it did not seem to be too long before Mom appeared to be doing better. I was 240 miles away and was only home to visit every couple of months. For me, the time flew by quickly. Plus, I was struggling through my own pain of Dad's death.

In reality, grief is not what it appears to be on the surface, and in hindsight it took me longer than I would have expected to find closure from my dad's death. I just couldn't see the forest for the trees.

Zig Ziglar, one of the greatest motivation gurus of all time and a devout Christian, said, "If there were no love, there'd be no grief." If you have a heart, grief will be nipping at your heels, and periodically it takes a big bite out of your leg.

About a year and a half after Deborah died, a buddy called. We talked about the challenges of life. He shared that another friend had very recently lost his wife. The guy wanted to quit his job and go away, just shut down for a while. He was in a world of hurt.

I understood full well his emotional state. I felt the same way, but I couldn't quit. I wanted to check out, but I had too many obligations and promises to fulfill; and checking out was not an option. Maybe that was part of God's plan. Sometimes quitting is too easy and rarely does it solve our problems.

My buddy was telling me about his other friend's struggles and then said, "You seem to be doing pretty good."

"Really?" That was news to me. I had to remind my buddy that he didn't see me that often and that the cycle of each day, each week, and each month held its share of difficulties. I reminded him that he was not riding along with me on the gusts of pain, despair, loneliness, and hopelessness.

In the storm of grief, there are also waves of mental, emotional, and physical fatigue. You might be busy with the details of life, but the waves are still pounding the shores of your mind. You can hear at full volume the pounding waves when you relax a bit or have some quiet time. The storm is raging wildly even if no one else can see or hear it, and you have no energy to try to fight against the waves. Up against the rocky shoreline, you feel overwhelmed to the point of drowning.

Have you ever sat down and talked heart to heart with someone grieving the loss of a close loved one? I mean, have you ever had a deep and open conversation, listening to what they are really saying or even asking some penetrating questions about how they are truly doing?

My guess is that you haven't. Experience tells me that most of the time our conversations are somewhat shallow—talking about the fluff of day-to-day life, things that really don't matter so much in the overall scheme of life.

Bill: "Hey Joe. How are you?"

Joe: "Doing fine! How are you, Bill?"

Bill: "Excellent."

And the charade goes on, two well-meaning guys hiding the truth from each other. We have all heard speeches and sermons or read about being transparent and honest. Why is it such a struggle?

I bet, more times than not, the Joes and Bills of the world are being disingenuous, hiding behind a mask of unreality, not being honest with themselves and others. In Susan Cain's book *Quiet: The Power of Introverts in a World that Can't Stop Talking*, Cain talks about the extrovert ideal. This is the concept that says that our ideal self is gregarious, alpha, and comfortable in the spotlight. We just need to show a positive face and a positive attitude. Create your own reality by how you speak. My dad would say bull———t!

Part of it may be pride. Pride goes before the fall, and sometimes we have to fall hard to be prepared to face reality. The problem with pride is that it blinds you to the reality around you and the reality of who you are. Denial is also easy and works, at least for a time.

Sometimes fear plays a role: the fear of confronting our pain and its root cause. Maybe we're afraid of facing some old wounds that are just too difficult to confront or let go of. I think we are afraid to ask how someone else is really doing out of fear of not knowing what to do or say if we find out there's real pain. Truth scares us.

Then there are the times I think we just forget about other

people's pain with all the busyness in our own lives. It's a frantic and complex world, and it takes a lot of our energy to stay engaged with our own challenges let alone remember someone else's. But if we say someone is a friend and we care about them, then we should try to truthfully engage in their lives amidst our busyness.

So, when does someone have closure from the most gut-wrenching circumstances of life?

About ten years before I met Deborah, I briefly dated a neat woman who had been married in her early twenties and widowed early. After a number of dates, I felt something blocking the development of a relationship.

Long after our last date, it hit me: She was still not over the loss of her husband. After a period of fifteen or more years, she still did not have closure. I'm not even sure she knew this. That's a tough place to find yourself, if indeed you ever realize it.

People mean well. About six months after Deborah died, an old girlfriend from high school wanted to set me up on a date with one of her friends. Other people would ask if I had started dating yet. Half the time I wanted to puke (figuratively speaking). Usually, I would just start missing Deborah all the more. Either way, at the time, these well-meaning efforts left me in an emotionally painful place. Closure was a long way off.

An usher friend from church had lost his spouse a few years earlier. They had been married for a long time. She was wheelchair bound for many of those years; he was devoted to taking care of her. One day, out of the blue, he told me that it could take up to five years to heal from the loss of a spouse.

Then about a month later I ran into a lady who used to have an office in my building. She let me know how sorry she was for my loss of Deborah and that her husband had died almost five years earlier. She said she still missed him dearly.

Two people, totally unknown by each other, and they are both telling me the same thing. This rocked me.

Five years? Could this much pain really last five years? Don't people get over the loss of a spouse way faster?

I was learning by personal experience and from friends that closure was not so quick and easy. The pain of Deborah's loss subsided some over time but in fits and spurts. And little things—holidays, anniversaries, reunions—could cause the pain to return in intense ways.

Even going to church could cause a flood of difficult emotions; a certain song, a specific Bible passage, or the pastor's sermon could easily trigger the pain. I would go down front to sit at Bible study just so I wouldn't see all the happy couples walking in. It hurt deeply to see their joy and feel only my emptiness.

Once in a while, without warning, I'd get blindsided by a really bad day, which felt like a belly crawl through molasses.

Part of closure involves moving past the pain, and the time that it takes is unique for each of us. We are each wired differently and have different life experiences. The point is not to make assumptions that everyone's journey is the same or what you perceive it should be, especially if you have never traveled down this path.

Certainly, each person's experience and circumstances are different when losing a loved one. I have heard of people being remarried within a year of a spouse's death. On the flip side I have heard of people for whom it takes many, many years to find closure, and some never get there.

I asked Rick about this during a counseling visit a couple of years after Deborah's death. "Why does it still hurt so much?"

He suggested it might be due to the intensity of our relationship and short time together. Deborah and I had not been with each other very long, and it almost seemed like we did not have a chance to really get to know each other the way couples do who have been married a lifetime. But one thing is for sure, our relationship was intense.

When things were good between Deborah and I, they were intensely good, as good as I had ever hoped and dreamed. But when things were off-kilter, our relationship was intensely difficult, uglier than anything I could have ever imagined. Our marriage had a whipsaw aspect. The joys and pains of our relationship were on such opposite ends of the spectrum you would think it impossible to survive. And it nearly was!

Maybe Rick was on to something. The pain of Deborah's loss was so difficult because our relationship was so intense. But it goes deeper yet.

Why is closure so difficult?

I believe we are hardwired for relationships. We were created to interact and bond with fellow humans at a level far beyond what any other creature in the animal kingdom experiences. Our relationships with each other are intensely deep and soulful, especially with our family and those with whom we are most emotionally entwined.

When our relationships are fractured, whether by divorce, fights, or even forced separation (like a soldier leaving his family for a tour of duty), there is pain and grief. That pain is often intense, and the more intense, the longer it takes to heal. For some, the wounds never heal. Each time Deborah and I had a fight, there was new pain and fractures in our relationship.

What happens when our relationships are terminated by death? The intensity of our grief and pain is magnified because the separation is permanent. The finality feels shattering. When our love for someone is intense, the pain of their loss is equally intense. When this separation happens suddenly with no chance to prepare or say goodbye or say I'm sorry, the anguish can be debilitating. That is where I was mentally and emotionally the day Deborah died, and I had flashbacks of my conversation with Kenna.

It was often during times like these that this Bible passage from the speech by Lt. Clebe McClary, way back in 1988, came to mind:

> [W]e . . . rejoice in our suffering because we know that suffering produces perseverance; perseverance, character; and character, hope. And hope does not disappoint us, because God has poured out his love into our hearts by the Holy Spirit, whom he has given us.
>
> —Romans 5:3–5 NIV

That hope was my anchor, and it was the same hope Deborah had.

God answered Deborah's prayers. He also answered mine, just in a different way than I envisioned.

AFTERWORD

THE SOURCE FOR CLOSURE

"God moves in a mysterious way, His wonders to perform.
He plants his footsteps in the sea, and rides upon the storm."

—William Cowper

Not only are we hardwired for relationships with each other, but we are also wired for relationship with God. All of us, to one degree or another, have a fractured relationship with God. Skeptics or atheists will try to deny this, but if you really dig down deep with them, you will find that for many of them they are angry toward God for some perceived injustice. They hurt in their relationship with God just like they do with any other person they shared conflict with, and they suppress this hurt by denying God or by blaming God for certain things that have happened in their life. It's the same pain process.

Have you ever been around someone who vehemently denies the existence of God? I have. And it's not so much that they don't believe in God, but that they have a visceral hatred toward God caused by intense pain. Often, it is hard to get them to divulge what happened in the past that caused this rupture in their relationship with the Almighty.

Recognizing the fallibility of each other ideally should help us find healing in our fractured relationships, but, unfortunately, reconciliation and closure too often never happens because anger, resentment, pride, fear, denial, jealousy, and a host of other emotions block the path to healing relationships.

When will I find closure from Deborah's death? I don't know, but there is good news. There is a means to complete and everlasting closure.

Deborah came to understand this after her dad died. Sometime after his death, Deborah became a Christian. She recognized that her most important relationship was with God and that only Jesus could bring closure to that fractured relationship, here and now and forever.

Deborah chose Jesus and found the source for closure. Jesus personally offers each of us a free gift: the gift of peace with God and a healed and complete relationship with Him.

Think of the greatest gift you ever received, whether it was for Christmas or a birthday. No doubt that brings back some great memories. I especially remember Christmas as a small kid. I remember the gifts waiting for me beside the Christmas tree. The anticipation and excitement almost left me incoherent, and when the gifts were finally opened, I was not disappointed.

Whatever your greatest gift was, it can't compare to the free gift that Jesus offers each of us, if only we accept it.

Even when accepting this gift, our relationships in this life can still remain fractured. Deborah did not have perfect relationships with many people, and the same is true of me. Our relationship was at times intensely fractured. However, she knew that through Jesus, one day we would be together again and experience the most astounding and perfect relationship beyond our finite worldly comprehension.

Deborah was presented with a choice, and she chose Jesus and secured her eternal peace with God.

On Sunday, August 29, 2010, Deborah was presented complete and everlasting closure.

> *There is no condemnation,*
> *There is no hell for me,*
> *The fire and the torment*
> *My eyes shall never see;*
> *For me there is no sentence,*
> *For me death hath no sting*
> *Because the Lord who loves me*
> *Shall shield me with His wing.*

—Paul Gerhardt

What's your choice? Do you want closure and the peace that surpasses all understanding?

You can travel along this life denying—or more likely you are just ignoring—God, like the atheist. Or you may scoff or laugh off this God and Jesus thing. I understand that attitude and thought process is prevalent in our society. The media, our educational system, and our culture in general denigrate and ridicule religion, especially Christianity. But that does not change the reality we will all face one day.

My Bible study teacher often said, "You can choose your actions or you can choose your consequences, but you can't choose both." The actions or choices you make in this life set the course for your eternal destiny. Once you die, your consequences are set; they are irrevocable and can never be changed. Therefore, you must choose wisely now.

You admit there is a spiritual reality to life and a god of some form. You then may ask, "Why Jesus and the God of the Bible?" My personal answer is reason and logic**,** and faith!

The best definition of faith I have come across is, "Faith is active trust in what you have good reason to believe is true."

Many people claim, and many other people believe, that

all religions lead to the same end. If you study the religions of the world and are intellectually honest with yourself, you will find that this is a logical fallacy. The religions of the world invariably teach different concepts and conflicting viewpoints.

Christianity, Islam, Buddhism, Hinduism, Mormonism, Shinto, Taoism, atheism, and all the other world religions cannot all be true at the same time. Some teach there is no reality, while another teaches there is a god and you must perform certain works to make him happy, to be approved. Others teach that we are each a god or goddesses, or part of the divine whole—the cosmic consciousness.

The variations and contradictions of the world's religions are vast and complex. An honest and curious person will realize they cannot all be the same means to the same end. All roads do not lead to Rome! That is the reasoned conclusion if one makes a thorough study of the diverse religious philosophies. They could all be wrong, but they cannot all be true.

Jesus separates from the religions of the world. He confirms that there is an all-powerful and all-loving God. In short, if you understand there is a God and that you want peace with Him now and for eternity, you don't have to do anything but believe in Jesus. It's a free gift if you choose to accept it.

In the New Testament of the Bible, the fourth book is John, written by the disciple of Jesus who became known as the apostle John. In the book of John, Jesus says repeatedly to "believe in Me."

I disagree with Calvin Coolidge who said, "Persistence and determination alone are omnipotent." Like logic and reason, they will get you only so far in life and then you hit a brick wall. That's when the One who is omnipotent comes calling.

Jesus asks you to believe in Him and who He says He is: "I am the way, the truth, and the life. No one comes to the Father except through me" (John 14:6).

Some people don't accept this perceived exclusivity, but they can take that up with Jesus if they get the chance.

In the movie *Indiana Jones and the Last Crusade,* the main character, Indy, is in an ancient cavern filled with hundreds of chalices, one of which is supposed to be the cup Jesus used at the Last Supper. Indy must choose the correct cup in order to live. If he chooses the wrong cup, he dies. While contemplating his cup selection, Indy is told by the Grail Knight, "Choose wisely." That is exactly what each of us is tasked with in life.

Jesus offers you the peace that surpasses all understanding. Deborah and multitudes of others over millennia have accepted Jesus' offer. They believed. They chose Jesus and chose wisely. Will you?

Your time to decide is short.

A POEM
BY JOSH TAYLOR

Masses are chasing
Crowns of this world
Rushing, grasping, and racing

Proclaims the fool
Live for today
Eat, drink, and drool

Gangrenous, false bliss
Worldly crowns are
Yokes drawing to the abyss

Using heart and mind
Reason as your guide
Liberate from the grind

Open your ears
Stop, look, and see
Pursue that which endures

Truth is told
Insight from the Ancient
Yeshua the Crown—seek and hold

Skeptic can deny
Their choice firm
Oh the eternal cry!

ACKNOWLEDGMENTS

Any story and the writing of the related book is not a one-man show. Many people are involved and are due thanks.

All my thanks to:

Dainah Craft, who was always available and kept me from a complete and breakdown in the midst of the storm;

Our counselors Rick Ghent and Kenna Barron for all their skill and care;

Ginger Freeman for her hours proofreading the early manuscript;

Mike Klassen and his Illumify Media team who helped get this book to print;

My cousin Michelle Denker-Sis, who created the cover art, understanding exactly what I was requesting;

Laura Matthews of thinkStory.biz, who helped with last-minute editing;

My great friends Marty Fye and Nick Newey, who regularly reached out during the long dark time after Deborah's departure;

Otto, the miniature Schnauzer, who kept me out of the pit of despair with his infectious excitement (dogs truly are a man's best friend, and Otto is the best of the best);

Pastor Dix Winston, who I went to several times for help and who told me, "You need to write this down. People need to know your story";

And finally, thanks to Jesus the creator and sustainer of this world and my Savior.